HAPPILY HERE AFTER

What the Animals want your heart to know

Angèle Deane

TABLE OF CONTENTS

INTRODUCTION

"There are only two ways to live your life. One is as though nothing is a miracle. The other is that everything is a miracle".
— Albert Einstein

If you are hurting or longing to know more about what happens to the animals when they leave us, then I write this for you, beautiful soul. If I were face to face with you, you would be able to feel my heart and my hope is that you can imagine me sitting there with you, sharing with you what I know. You would see that my eyes light up when I talk about the animals and to me it is all a miracle.

It is one of the hardest moments we have to endure in this human experience to say goodbye to our animals. It is the purest love we share with another living being and the saddest goodbye.

This isn't the end of the line as some may want you to believe. This could be the start of your learning journey in discovering what is true for you. It could be a greater understanding of your relationship with your animal, a deeper connection with yourself and being open to your own miracles and a realisation that our connection continues after they pass.

Maybe you have had concerns about your decisions or choices for your animal leading up to their passing? You may be wondering if your animal forgives you? Perhaps you are wondering where they are and what they are doing? You may be wondering and wanting to know if they are ok?

Have you had suspicions that you felt your animal on your bed as you slept? Did you hear your cat's meow after they passed? Maybe it was your dog's soft whine, yet he is no longer here in body? Are you considering getting another animal and don't know if it is the right thing? Do you wonder if your animal in Spirit will be upset? In my work as an animal communicator, these are some of the heartfelt questions I hear often with people about their animals.

I have been blessed with helping the animals and their people. Part of my work is to be a voice for the animals that have crossed over or as I like to say, in Spirit. It has been a real gift to be able to bring peace and comfort to those who are hurting after they have had to say goodbye to their animals. My life is sprinkled with miracles in my journey with the people and the animals I have had the honour of being of service with. I have also experienced loss with my own animals, and one might think that because this is part of my work as an animal communicator that in some way it might be easier, I promise you, it isn't.

I ask that you be curious while reading this book. Have an open mind and an open heart and you will be in the right heart set to recognise signs from your animal in Spirit. If and when you do receive a sign from your animal, or have a feeling they are around or have returned, it won't be dismissed as a fluke or wishful thinking, coincidence or crazy. You will know it was your animal and yes the sign they gave, was just for you. The beautiful thing is, if it begins with curiosity, a seed of possibility is planted.

Think of this time as sacred and just for you. You may just have your animal beside you in Spirit as you read. Your analytical mind can take a break for a moment, you can go right back to it when you finish reading, but all I ask is that while you read, you feel with your heart first.

I want you to know it's ok to cry and I am so very sorry you are hurting. If I were to sit with you in person, I would ask you if I could tell you what I know about the animals. You might want to share with me something that you think others may think was crazy or woo woo and I would tell you, share away anyway! We would discover together that it isn't crazy after all but a miracle just for you. That is how our conversation together would begin, as we explore what this means for the animals to be Happily Here After.

Within these pages, I will share my learnings and stories from my own personal experience as an animal communicator. I see myself as a student of life, I am always learning and my hope is, by me sharing what I know up until now, it may just help a hurting heart that wants to know more about the animals in Spirit. This may be you who is reading and if it is, then these words from my heart are for you.

Throughout the book I will share examples from the animals and their people. Please know that the experiences within this book can happen with any kind of animal and is not limited to the animals in the stories. I chose these stories to give you evidence of what can be possible. Although I have changed names for privacy of my clients, the actual events and stories are true. I want you to know that you are not alone, and we are all connected to each other through our hearts not only through loss, but also in healing. The common thread that exists for all who read this book, is the love that we all have for our animals.

I would like to clarify my use of the word transition when referring to your animal in spirit. I don't say died or dead when referring to your animal that has passed. I say the word transitioning. I say this because I know that we are all energy. I know that energy never dies it only changes form. As the physical body is completing this cycle, I do say dying as the form is ending and changing into another. I say the term in Spirit for the realm that they are in and not heaven simply because when I say in heaven, I immediately think of up there or away from us somewhere else. For me, I know it's here. I know they are no longer physical yet still very much living, so I say in Spirit for this.

I don't use the word pet either when referencing the animals, for the simple fact that I know that you have been chosen by them just as much as you have chosen them. The animals are our companions, our family members. I also don't use the word owner. I see humans and animals co- existing as equals, though of course, not the same as the animals.

Our journey with the Animals will begin with you getting to know who I am and how my life changed when I said goodbye to my soul dog. I want you to know I understand and though my experience is uniquely mine, you will know that my heart hurt just like yours.

Your heart is healing after experiencing loss and we will look at ways that you can help yourself as you heal. I will show you how the animals are checking in on you and know what you do to remember them. Your heart is also a very important part of the connection with your animal, we will discuss how this is.

Your soul is guiding you as you are having a human experience, I will share with you how to recognise this guidance. Just as your soul has unique guidance just for you, so does your heart. Your way of connecting with animals and knowing when they are sending you signs begins with learning the language of the heart. I will share with you how your imagination and intuition are so very important in connecting with your animals. Recognising the various ways information can come to us will help you understand why sometimes what you feel to be true to your heart does not always make sense to your head.

I will share how the animal that was with you is unique and they have their own soul purpose in coming to be with you. The animals have shown me how they perceive life and their experience of being in pure energy form. They are not anywhere but here and I will share with you how they let their people know they are here with the signs they send. You may recognise a sign your own animal has sent your way.

We will look into soul agreements that the animals can have with their people. Not every animal returns and the animals have explained why this is and how time is irrelevant when they choose to return. Soul overs and walk ins will be explored so you can recognise what it is and when and if it happens for you.

I will share with you amazing accounts of animals returning and what you can do to be sure you find them. You will discover it isn't by you doing anything but more of a way of being and your intention. Your animal in Spirit can be included in the choosing of another animal and they assist. We will explore how they can do this and how to prepare yourself and other animals to welcome a new animal home.

When our hearts are hurting and we have experienced this hurt, it needs our attention and our care. It can transform us from the inside if we are open to it. We can reconnect with parts of ourselves that we may have left behind or forgotten and to use this time and hurt to gently move us forward as we heal. No pushing or pretending will help this process. This takes honesty and courage. Acknowledging what you are really feeling and what you need takes honesty, it takes courage to follow through in taking care of yourself and accepting how it is on any given day.

Grief is a journey, albeit one we wish we never had to experience. It can be unsettling to say the least, inconvenient with tears or that gulp in your throat. We may tend to think that grief is happening to us and something we must get through. I want to share with you that this can be a transformative time for you as you heal.

x

Come join me as I share with you what I know and maybe your heart can open again or open up even more and you can find a new way of experiencing life and your animals.

BEGINNINGS

Anything and everything you have experienced has been purposeful, it has brought you to where you are now.
— Inyanla Vansant

I haven't always been an animal communicator, though my love for animals has certainly always been there. My very first friendship at age three, happened to be with a boxer dog named Fritzi. It was every bit as real as being friends with another human three-year-old. No one told me you can't be best friends with an animal, so I didn't know any different.

The only thing was, Fritzi didn't use words. You don't need a whole lot of words at age three, she just got me, and I got her. It never really changed when it came to any other animal as I got older.

With every animal I have met throughout my life, I have always known they are a unique personality and character. I honestly see it as meeting another being with their own likes and interests and way of seeing things. I have always had animals around me and have had some amazing encounters with them. If I ever was or am at a gathering or at someone's home, I will be the one that scans at knee height or below for any animals I can meet.

I love people too, so it is very rewarding for me to meet the beautiful people I do, alongside their animals. I have always loved helping people recognise their ability to heal themselves and to encourage them to be who they are. I studied counselling and therapy and this has brought so much value in my work with people and the animals.

I had the most vivid imagination when I was a child. Anytime I was able to, I would be drawing or painting. One of my favourite things to do would be to turn an ordinary situation into something exciting. This gift of imagination has stayed with me and we all have it and in this book, I will explain why it is important for you, not just for the animals but for your everyday life.

I have a very soft spot for children, especially toddlers and I worked in Montessori education. I loved every minute of my time working with the children, it was a very fulfilling role. I stopped when I became a parent and turned my attention to raising my own children. Now, I am a mum to three beautiful girls with my amazing husband. Animals have always been a part of our family. Throughout our life together, we have had cats, rats, lizards, a bird, a snake, dogs, guinea pigs and at this moment, we have three dogs in our family.

I am an artist and have a studio tucked in my backyard right next to the pool, where my dogs accompany me when I am being creative. I love doing all sorts of artistic and creative work, including portraits of the animals. You will find me in the studio painting, creating or writing when I am not connecting with the animals or people.

Spirituality has always been close to my heart. The religion I was raised in brought me much pain and anxiety however, I realised throughout it all, that I did have a love for Spirituality and was very aware I was not alone. I always felt that I was being taken care of. I am forever grateful that it has been this way because it helped so much when at age 21, I lost my Dad to terminal illness. My whole world turned upside down.

Have you ever felt uncomfortable with your whole life? It can happen after a huge life changing event. Have you experienced it where you question everything and nothing feels right anymore? You don't necessarily know what would feel right either? So, you begin searching for ways to feel some kind of normal and comfortable again in your life. That was me.

No longer feeling right with the beliefs I was raised with; I began to question everything I thought I knew. Everything was examined and tested as to whether it felt true for me or not. I began my learning journey and learnt all I could in personal development and Spirituality. I began finding my truth and applied all I knew to my everyday life.

I learnt to listen to my intuition and trust my own inner guidance. All that no longer fit or felt true for me had to go. My beautiful Mum was diagnosed with Alzheimer's as I was having my second daughter. We went through the painful and gradual loss of my mum as we were raising our girls. It was a cruel loss and left my heart raw. As you can see, I am no stranger to loss or grief. My introduction to really trusting non-verbal communication and listening with my heart and intuition played a very important part in my Mum's illness. She became non-verbal, so using this skill in learning to listen differently, helped in continuing communication and having a connection with her.

Throughout the years including today and hopefully for the remainder of my days, I am constantly learning and studying. In my everyday life, I am an animal communicator, psychic, therapist, artist and author and work with both people and animals. It's a very full life I live, I love every minute of it. I have my soul dog Gordon to thank. You will learn more about Gordy but for now, I will say that when we lost our boy, I was so lost and wanted answers on the afterlife of animals. I had so many questions, would he come back to me ever? Could he? Where is he?

There is a lot of information out there and just as each person has their own perspective and experience, so it is with the information they share. It was discernment that got me through the sea of information and found what was true for me. As I discovered what I did about the animals, I was relieved to learn that there is an Afterlife and you really can communicate with animals, I had the strongest feeling that this might be something I could do as well. The best way to know if you can do something or not, is to get in there and just do it. I started practicing in a group setting, online with other people's animals, I discovered that animal communication was my thing and felt so natural for me.

While practicing, people were coming to me often, asking me to connect with their animals. I became busy as one person told another. My clientele grew and today I am blessed to have genuine connections with animals and people all over the world.

Connecting with the animals on an energetic level in communications, I started to see people that weren't supposed to be there. I would describe the personality and details about a person, only to learn that the person had passed and was in Spirit. I knew and said things before they happened with the animals and their people. I would then have confirmations that they did actually happen.

During this time, I learnt that every single person is on their own unique journey in whatever field they are in. Mine included. I decided to take any limitations off me from others who decided you can't do this or do that or that can't happen. I had to find out what I could and couldn't do, what could and couldn't happen but most importantly, what felt right for me. My biggest challenge was to accept myself as I am.

I used to be so worried what would people think if they knew what I could do? Who do I think I am to write a book now? Now, my love for the animals and what I do, is so much greater than my fears and there is work to do. I am being a voice for the animals the best way I know how.

I don't want you to think that I think, I have all the answers. I know I don't. I am a person like you, doing exactly what I love. I have seen and experienced some amazing things along the way. I want to share with you what I believe are glimpses into the Afterlife. I call them glimpses because I don't think anyone can really know how it really is, or have a complete picture, until we get there for ourselves. I feel it is too immense and out of our scope of understanding with our human minds.

I have the strongest sense that it can't be the same for everyone when it is our time to go. Life here on earth is an individual experience for each person with our own perspectives and meaning. I feel it is the same with the Afterlife. I don't feel as though where the animals are, is that far away, like the other side or up there. I feel as though it is right here, although in a different form. I want to show you, just how close the animals are to us. Mostly though, I want you to know you are loved and your animal is still connected to you and communicating with you.

FOR THE LOVE OF GORDON

How lucky am I to have something that makes saying goodbye so hard
– Winnie The Pooh; AA Milne

You now know, I have experienced huge losses in my life, both human and animals. I want to share with you who Gordon is, his importance to me in my life and in my journey in animal communication. It is all because of him, that I am doing this now.

Gordy is my soul dog. I love all my animals but there was an incredible connection with Gordon and I from the first time I laid eyes on him. You will absolutely know what I mean if you have felt this connection. I knew him and he knew me. Before I share this with you, this is NOT the way to get a dog. I am going to put this down to pregnancy and perhaps stubbornness on my behalf because logic went completely out the window with this decision, I am forever grateful every day that it did.

You see, I was five months pregnant with our first daughter. Here we are, a young couple on a single income and getting ready for our new arrival. This one morning, I get inspired with thinking how nice it would be to get a dog to grow up with our baby girl. A puppy would be best.

Thinking back on how I grew up with dachshunds in my own childhood, I thought a dachshund puppy would be even cuter. My search began.

I found a black and tan pup online, 10 weeks old. He was in another state and would need to be transported but I thought, not to worry, I would figure all that out. It felt so right, so I called to enquire about him. I had so many questions and all of them were answered. He was the one! My intuition knew this but I still had my husband to convince. It took me three hours of me answering all of his questions. Surprisingly, it was a yes and yes, I have one of the best husbands in the world to this day.

When all was said and done, Gordon was on his way to us. People told us we were crazy to do this now with a baby on the way. I could see their point but they didn't know me well enough though. They had no idea what I was prepared to do to have this puppy be a part of our family.

I have never jumped around so happily as much as that evening when we got the call that Gordon had arrived and we could pick him up!

The people that transported him from Sydney had arrived at our agreed location and we could go and pick him up! The excitement was immense! The moment I held this pup, I burst into tears, I loved him already! He was my boy! I kissed his head and his huge paws! I played with his long velvety ears and began telling him how perfect he was, which led me to telling him how every inch of him was pure perfection.

Gordon grew into a strong 18 kilo standard dachshund. He was all muscle, his chest puffed out proudly. He was one of the biggest dachshunds in our area. He was the boss dog of our home and family. Throughout his lifetime, Gordy welcomed all our daughters into the world. He was with me through two miscarriages and was by my side through the diagnoses and progression of Alzheimer's with my mum. He went through the loss of her with me. This boy was my source of unconditional love through all the hard parts of life and though my heart would feel so broken sometimes, every single time I looked at him, I would smile the truest of smiles.

Of course he loved everyone in the family, he had a special purpose with each of us but this connection between him and I was undeniable. He was incredibly loyal and always by my side. Every time I left the house, he would wait for me. Any room I was in, there was Gordon. He was my second in charge, he had to know everything that was going on and if I corrected my daughters, he would have a say too, as if to back me up!

14 years we were gifted with him in our lives. Through those years, he was the very best teacher for the girls in learning how to be a respectful caretaker and how to love a dog. Our family had so many laughs as I would be the voice of Gordon, imagining what he was saying. I would say what I thought out loud. I felt so connected to him. Imagine my surprise when I learnt through discovering animal communication, that what I thought could be something Gordon would say, was actually from Gordon and here I was, thinking I was guessing, pretending and playing.

Gordon became very sick at 13 years old. We had just returned from a four-week holiday away and had to take him to a vet. He had an enlarged heart and heart disease. We had medication to keep the fluid down in his body but over the next 12 months, he progressively got worse.

We got to his 14th birthday. I had a feeling it would be his last one. It was a major milestone for me, I don't know why really. Perhaps I was thinking if he could reach that milestone, he could defy other odds too. I was so proud of him but what kind of condition was he in and what life was he living to get there?

There came a morning where I had to get Gordon to the vet to have the fluid drained from his body, due to the inflammation around his heart. It usually was once a month at this point but this time, the time frame was much shorter. I would take Gordy, his belly full of water and it was so very heavy for him. When he would come back, he would be so much lighter and happier but when I looked at him after the last visit, I asked myself, 'When did he get so bony?' I could see so clearly how taxing this was on his body and his pride was hurting.

I was getting ready to go and pick Gordon up from the vets. I just knew in my heart, that the vet was going to say something about it being his time. Throughout his life, any thought or mere mention of Gordon not being here with me, would bring me to tears and this was no different. The vet had decided to do a scan of Gordon's heart on this day and she was shocked at the size of his heart. She expressed to me that Gordon was living on sheer love. By no means at all, should he be physically able to be alive in this condition. Looking at the images, the size of Gordon's heart was enormous in comparison to a normal size heart. We never would have known about this had she not have given him a scan that day.

I sat my daughters down when we got home and let them know what had been said at the vets. Two weeks after this appointment, his medication had run out. I knew in my heart that it was time. I asked for a confirmation from the Universe somehow to let me know that it was the right decision. I wanted to focus on something else than what was happening with Gordon. I turned my attention on the book I was reading at the time. I sat quietly and read, only to come across a paragraph in the book. I gasped out loud as I read! It literally read 'Walking up the stairs with Archangel Michael represented Gordon ascending to another place- some would call it heaven.' I burst into tears. There was my confirmation.

Going against everything within me, I called the vet and was shaking and crying as I made the appointment. The vet would be coming to our house to assist Gordon. We had just two days left with Gordy. Every part of me hated every single minute leading up to this.

The morning of April 5th 2017 was a quiet morning. I woke up early and sat with Gordon and gave him cuddles telling him today was the day that he would be pain free. He looked at me deep in my eyes as if to say, 'Yes I know and I am ok'. He happily ate his breakfast and we gave Gordy his favourite treats. Cream cheese, salami, dog treats, whatever he wanted!

We went through the motions of the morning, my heart pounding every second and the pit of my stomach was so heavy and filled with dread. Every inch of me didn't want this to happen but there was no way out. It was during school holidays, so all my girls were home and having quiet moments with Gordy. I set up his bed in the living room exactly how Gordon liked it, complete with his favourite blanket.

The children of our street and neighbours as well as family, all dropped by to say goodbye to Gordon. He wasn't just a dog in our life, he was family and a friend. Not once did Gordon think you were coming by to see the people in his home. You were allowed to come in on one condition, pats and scratches for him first and then people.

Molly our cat had come into our room the previous night and sat next to Gordon for around 20 minutes. They had their conversation, when they were finished, she got up and left the room.

Sylvie our Lhasa Apso and Gordon's little sister, both sat in the doorway of our home and I watched them both as Gordon slowly scanned the front of the house. I was sweeping as he did this and he looked up at my face intently. I stopped and smiled at him. Sweeping was all I could think of doing while counting down the minutes til the vet arrived at 11am. I now know, I got to see and be a part of Gordon's heart snapshot. I will share with you exactly what this is a bit later.

The vet came with an assistant, they shared a few days later that it wasn't easy for them to go through this with us. Gordon welcomed them in like a true gentleman and then went and sat on his bed and waited. He was so calm. Everyone was gathered around him. I was comforting my youngest daughter as Gordon strained his neck to look to see where I was. I came and lay down next to him and he got comfortable and tucked his head under my arm, as he always did since a puppy whenever he wanted to feel safe.

I said a little prayer for Gordon, asking the angels to lead him straight to the treats table on arrival. I thanked Gordy for being the amazing boy he is and for all the love we shared together for his whole life. We all had our hands on our boy as he took his final breath.

That afternoon, my daughters and I were all laying on our bed just being with each other as we cried. I have a white ceiling fan above my bed and I looked up with tears in my eyes. As I looked up, there in the reflection, was a shape like Gordon under the crook of my arm. What!!! I showed the girls. Each daughter was saying 'It's Gordy! It's Gordy!' There he was in the ceiling fan reflection right beside me. Yet if I looked at my actual side, nothing. We stared at the ceiling fan for the longest time. I have since thanked Gordon, now knowing what I know, confirmed what we experienced is very real.

That night, I lay in the living room long after everyone had gone to bed. Finally, I could just feel all my sadness after comforting my daughters through their sadness. As I lay there with my eyes full of tears, I saw a golden ball go right in front of my face. I just looked at it and thought to myself 'Wow, a golden ball!' Amazed, I watched it as it slowly arced in front of me, as if in slow motion. It didn't even go away when I was looking at it directly. What is this? Could this also be Gordy?

So, my journey into finding answers and some peace of mind began over the next few weeks. Nothing seemed to be bringing me peace or easing the hurt and emptiness I was feeling. How could I know that Gordon was ok? Could Gordon ever come back? Could I communicate with him? Did I communicate with him when he was here, is that how we were so connected and I just didn't realise? These questions and searching for the answers would bring me clarity to what my purpose was and how I could help others.

In my discoveries I slowly came across all different kinds of people and all different beliefs. I had to go through what felt true for me. I finally found my answers! I finally found my peace and calm about my loss of Gordon.

This was the time I came across animal communication once again. I say once again because I had read a few books years ago and was curious. I even practiced with Gordon but never pursued anything at that time. Coming across this once more, I joined an animal communication group online and did a few courses and then knew this is what I had been doing with Gordon and all the animals in my life the whole time.

This heart work really found me; I have Gordon to thank for that always.

I share my story about Gordy with you because to me, it's important for you, to get a feel for who I am. I know from experience what you may be feeling, though your experience and feelings are always uniquely yours. Our connection would be that I have a heart like you and hurt like you do and had to heal from the loss of animal just like you.

Your heart is one of the most important parts of this journey, so let's look at what you could be doing to help yourself during this vulnerable time.

TAKING CARE OF YOU WHILE REMEMBERING THEM

Grief can be the garden of compassion. If you keep your heart open through everything, your pain can become your greatest ally in your life's search for love and wisdom.
– Rumi

Your animal is no longer here to touch, hold, feel, play with, walk with, ride, however you spent time with your animal. They are now gone in the physical form. It hurts and it happened. I am so very sorry for your loss of your best friend, your soul animal and the pure love in action, that they gave you every single day with you.

We are conditioned to push ourselves forward and be strong and sure a moment will come when you are able to do this. This time of grief, however uncomfortable and however long, is a necessary part of the journey of healing and it is uniquely yours. No one else can do this for you and no one else can decide how to do this that is right for you or how to feel, nor can they determine how long this journey to healing takes.

Just as falling in love and being in a relationship with or grieving for a person is your very own experience, so it is with your relationship with your animal and this journey through grief. Grief changes who we are, it becomes a part of our experience.

There are different types of grief that we can experience. So you understand what you may be going through, let's take a look at each.

Anticipatory Grief.

This grief can begin quite a while before the animal passes, it is the sadness we feel knowing what is coming. It often arrives when your animal has been diagnosed with a terminal illness, the acknowledgement of the preciousness of time left with your animal. Each change you notice as your animal gets older can bring a sadness. When we plan our animal's final moments, the emotions that we feel can be just as intense as the grief after the transition.

Normal Grief.

As if there is anything normal about this, however there is a healthy way to experience loss. Still going through the gamut of emotions of anger, guilt, sadness and eventually coming to a place of acceptance, we can go through this at our own pace and find peace.

Disenfranchised Grief

This is a kind of grief that does not always receive acknowledgment. As real as it is, it is often minimised. This is when people say things like "It was just a dog." "You can always get another one."

This kind of grief is not fully recognised or validated by others.

When grief is not witnessed, it can feel even heavier. Not only are you hurting from your loss, you may also feel as though you have to justify why you are hurting.

When euthanasia is involved, it can feel even more isolating. You are carrying the weight of the decision. While others may see it as practical or necessary, you may feel enormous emotions in a way that is difficult to explain.

Traumatic Grief

Grief of this nature hits hard when an animal's loss is sudden. It could be an accident, an injury, or an aggressive illness. The shock can bring up intense emotions and in some cases with those that suffer PTSD it can trigger dysregulation. When the loss is abrupt, healing may take longer and need the assistance of deeper support.

If you feel you would benefit in seeing a professional, please take the time to choose one that feels right for you. Depression and anxiety deserve more time and attention in addition to your personal care. The pain of losing a loved one is life changing. In the early days you may find that the grief comes in big waves, you may feel heavy with sadness, or you may feel numb. I know you may feel as if your heart will break any second now. It feels uncomfortable and unpredictable at times. Who would have thought it would be like this? You may even ask if I am ever going to be ok again? I feel it is important to recognise that having this experience happen and for us to hurt in the way that we do, that we are not the same person. There has been a change. It could mean that you view life differently, it may mean that for now, you are much quieter in your way of being. It is all just as it is meant to be. You may just want to retreat for a while from life and when you are ready you will return.

There is a precious gift that is there for you as you go through this journey, it is the gift of acknowledgment of the love that you have for your animal and the integration of this love experienced.

If no one else is going to do this part for you then I want to make sure that you are doing all you can to help your heart heal. It may feel all jumbled and raw for you or you may have already begun your healing process or perhaps only now, you feel brave enough to face it.

Grief doesn't just go away; it doesn't matter to grief how much time goes by. In a split second you can open this wound again and will feel just as raw and hurt as when it first happened. Pushing it aside doesn't help either, it will show up in all kinds of ways until you decide to allow it to exist. If we can be brave enough to go through this part gently, we can truly allow it to be part of our life experience and felt all the way through. When it does make its presence known, it will hurt still, I believe it always does, however it will be more like an awareness and an ache to let you know you have loved deeply and truly.

It is important for you to be honest with yourself in how you are really feeling. You are allowed to feel as you do, when you do. There can be a blanket of embarrassment on top of all else you are feeling. Our society is thankfully improving but still we aren't always given time to process our loss. We can be met with insensitivity in comments from others and we may feel pressure to just keep going with our lives. If you can commit to be honest with yourself in how you feel, then this can also mean that you give yourself permission and safety to take care of yourself as you are feeling how you are. Everyone is going to be different in what they need to take care of themselves and how they feel. If you need to cry then cry, if you are angry, acknowledge it and express it but not on other people or living beings. Maybe you are exhausted and need to sleep? When we ignore or downplay what we really feel, we can run into trouble.

Do all you can to really look after yourself in all areas as you experience grief. You will not cry the whole time you are grieving. If you honour the tears, you will eat and cry, function and cry, sleep and cry. There are gaps and breaks in between crying and not feeling so good, to being at least feeling ok as we go through grief. Everyone has their very own personal experience of grief.

This is where we can choose to be brave and go with the waves of our personal journey through grief. This is why it cannot be the same for everyone, not the time frame or the feelings you experience is ever the same as anyone else.

The grief we experience can be more accepted when we know what it actually is and how we are feeling is justified. For some of you, you may be experiencing numbness, nothing at all and there may be guilt for not feeling anything. It may be disbelief, overwhelming sadness or an apathy. These reactions are normal following a loss.

Carers Fatigue

If you have been caring for your animal who has been sick for a long time you may be exhausted emotionally, mentally and physically. You may not even realise you could be experiencing carers fatigue. The watching, worrying and waiting can take a toll on you, it may hit even harder when there is empty space and all that is left is you. The silence and empty pockets of time can allow the fatigue to rise and what worked before in coping no longer exists. Recognising the signs of carers fatigue is important so you can take care of yourself in a way that helps you as you go through the grief.

The signs of carers stress or fatigue can be:

Physical

Feeling tired and run down even after having a rest. Having trouble falling asleep or waking up exhausted. There can be frequent headaches, body aches, tension in the body and a weakened immune system, this can result in more sickness.

Emotional

These signs show up with irritability and anger, feeling frustration, mood swings and snappiness. You may feel overwhelmed or feeling flat, or constantly worried. You may feel guilty about feeling relief with the passing of your animal. You may find yourself withdrawing from friends, family and doing things you used to enjoy. Losing interest in self-care can be an indication and increased use of alcohol or stress eating. If you feel this is you then please do find a professional to support you through this.

In my experience with the animals and their people, so many people tend to forget to take care of the basic physical needs we all have. No matter the type of grief or stress, you are hurting. To ensure you have a good solid foundation and the necessities are taken care of, there are simple questions you could ask yourself every day while you are healing but of course, we can do this for ourselves at any given time. This could be your care plan for yourself for your chosen time frame, only you can know what this time frame is. You may want to follow through closely with your plan for the next week or two and then check in and see whether there is capacity to allow yourself to get back to the usual rhythm of life.

Sometimes people find themselves with way too much time on their hands after their animal has gone. This can happen when an animal has been the focus with treatments, appointments, attention and care from the person. Now what is there to do with all this time? May I kindly suggest that you write down some things you may be interested in but could not do before? Perhaps this can be an opportunity to get to know yourself again. Your animal would want you to be to happy. For one client, her love for sailing was something she loved to do but couldn't because of the time and attention her cat would need from her. She felt she had to be home for him, it was this way until he transitioned. After he had transitioned, she explored the possibility of sailing once more and has since made it a part of her life again.

Have you eaten properly? Are you eating to nourish your body? Are you remembering to eat something? I know you can feel like not doing anything much, sometimes as you heal. Could you plan for something to eat and make it easy for when these times come? Simple foods at this time may be all you can do and that is totally fine. Just please ensure you are nourishing your body. It can be a mammoth effort some days to even think about food, let alone prepare food for the family so how can it be an easier process for now? It may be that you give yourself two- or three-weeks grace. You might lean into take away food, frozen meals or very simple meals. Keep it simple for this next part in time. Please keep guilt out of this. Only kindness, as you adjust to the changes. You can check in again when you start to feel like you are able to do more.

Are you sleeping? Sleep can be elusive when we are going through grief, staying awake long into the night, or not reaching the deepest healing state of sleep yet again. Have you set yourself up for a good night's sleep? Do you have a calm and soothing nighttime routine for yourself? Does it include a warm tea or cool water before sleep? Is it a relaxing bath or shower with your favourite soap? Are you putting away technology for a good amount of time before sleeping? Do you have something gentle to read before you sleep if reading is what you like to do? I would suggest lighter reading especially for this time, so your mind and nervous system can get ready for resting. Is your bed fresh and comfortable? Is your bedroom a sanctuary for sleep? Is it peaceful? Clean? Calm? Is the room dark enough? Are you warm or cool enough? Is there soft music playing? Are your pyjamas comfortable? Every detail matters at this point. Unfortunately, and luckily, no one else is going to do this for you.

Sometimes when everything stops and we are left with our thoughts, we can find ourselves in a flurry of overthinking. If your mind is overwhelmed, it could be an idea for you to have a notebook by your bed and put it all on paper before you sleep. Let it all out and then let it be. It can be as messy as you like, to get it out quickly. Try it. This is not feeling our way through or trying to work anything out about what we write. This is simply to get it out on paper until your head feels empty. We can keep ourselves wide awake thinking and thinking a thousand things in our minds, so this way, it is all out in front of you and your mind can be free to rest and dream.

Are you physically and energetically moving? How have you moved your body today? Did you give yourself a nice walk? A stretch? Exercise in any form? Some gentle movement can do wonders for us to feel better, it doesn't have to be strenuous or regimented cardio, simply move how your body is asking you to move. Can't hear it asking? Take a moment to tune in and question what might feel good in that moment? Is it a walk? A dance? Some yoga? A run? A big stretch? You already know what could feel good for you so take a moment to listen after you ask.

Are you getting enough sunshine? Have you been outside and in the sun today? Being outside in the sun is fresh air and letting the outside help us heal. Face up to the sun and letting it soak into your skin just for 20 minutes a day can be so healing. Grab a blanket and sit outside in the backyard if you have one, you know your animal used to sit in the sun when they were in body. It felt good for them, just as it will for you. Get comfortable and relax for this time. You can read, journal, even enjoy a drink while you take in some sun.

Are you allowing yourself time to heal? Have you given yourself permission to step out of life for a while as you heal? It can mean giving yourself the space to feel how you do without apology and without having to pretend to be ok to keep anyone else happy. Trying to look happy and ok when you are hurting so much on the inside is exhausting. Be kind to yourself and check in with yourself regularly to see how you are feeling and then you can determine what you are needing. You most probably have a busy life and might not see how to get a break or create the space. It may mean fewer social engagements for a little while or creating times where you can be on your own and give yourself permission to feel all that sits inside. It may be an hour to yourself, or a few days. You will know what it is you need. You are allowed to cocoon when you need and you are allowed to rest. You won't stay here for always, but it may be just what you need for now.

As a collective we have become more aware of mindfulness and our mindset, we have so many tools we can use to help us and now the awareness is shifting to the heart, we need to take care of our heart as well. Your emotional well-being is part of the foundation of your whole well-being. Your heart needs your care and full attention in your healing. Everyone wants to be happy. We may wish this part would just hurry up and move on and somehow skip all the messy bits. We know we are hurting and we cry with how much this all hurts, we may wish it was all over with already. What if we made compassion for ourselves, the main focus during this time? What if kindness in all ways to ourselves, became our number one priority? If there ever was a perfect time to do something like this, it is now. What does this look like for you? Anything that helps you feel better that is helpful and not harmful is totally acceptable. When you are feeling better, then you can look again at what may need to change. Right now though, the focus is to get you through this time, tears and all.

Honour the ending

What could happen if we could give ourselves permission to just be here at the ending for a moment? It's a big thing I know, to fully acknowledge the finality of it all. Allow yourself to feel it all. All emotions are valid.

As you remember your animal while your heart is hurting, you know love is there. This love is a big, huge immeasurable amount! Be brave and ask why is there love here? Why am I asking you to do this? When you do this, all the memories will come flooding through. The first time you held them, their eyes, their cuddles, their loyalty, their cute faces, oh the list goes on. Can you feel the love?

To create the love between you and your animal, there was happiness, joy, gratitude, frustration, sadness, hope, resolve just to name a few. Can you see it is all in there? All the emotions and feelings are there, not only sadness and grief. In this moment of ending, this uncomfortable vulnerability you might be feeling, deserves a place to feel, for you to think and heal. We owe it to ourselves to give ourselves the space and to take some time here. Feel the not so good feelings, so the better feelings can rise too. Give them all recognition and let them out. It took all of these emotions to create the love and all of these emotions are within our grieving as well.

What if when you allowed yourself to feel it all, you also promised yourself to finish up with gratitude? It may sound something like this "My heart is literally breaking right now, and I am hurting so badly AND I am grateful that you aren't hurting anymore. Or it could be, I am so angry with how it all happened AND I am grateful that I am much clearer on what I will not ever allow to have happen again."

If we take the time to reflect on our life with our animal, we can acknowledge all of what we feel and come to a place of acceptance for all that happened. This part of your journey has come to an end so give it a warm place in your heart, wrapped in gratitude.

It can be difficult to accept what has happened that resulted in the loss of your animal, it can be the hardest part with feelings of anger and guilt. It may feel so final to admit and accept that this part of the journey is over. When you hurt as you remember, I am going to gently remind you also have another gift in there and you get to use this gift right away. You can use it to soothe your hurt as you are remembering and healing. I am talking about the gift of memories.

No one else has the memories that you have with your animal, not even the other family members or people in your lives. In fact, no one else has the same relationship that you have with your animal. You get to choose at any given time, any memory that can bring them back to you in your present moment. It is not about denying the sadness we feel, it is there all the same, but we can add to it. You can choose to pull up a memory of your animal that makes you smile and say AND I can remember this as well.

If I ask you to close your eyes and recall your animal, their beautiful eyes and face, what do you see? There they are right? It happened instantly and where are you right now? Here. So this one way we can bring the animal into this present moment and just be here for a minute with this.

As humans we have our memories and our perceptions, thankfully we have a way of capturing a memory for always. When we share with someone an experience we had or about someone we have met, we are telling a story. When we record or write down an experience or story, it is like a photograph in words, to capture all that was felt and experienced in that moment. It is your hand that is writing this, your feelings you are expressing about this moment. It is from your heart you remember your animal.

When sharing a story with someone else, it can bring a connection to another person in both of your experiences as a human being. You share a smile, a hug or a response with another person, it brings an exchange, a feeling of understanding and connection. Stories have been passed down through the human experience for all time. Writing and speaking in storytelling bring the stories to life while being listened or read in that moment. For that moment everyone present is immersed in their imagination as they bring meaning to what they hear or read.

I know you have stories about your animal, they are all inside of you. What if you shared a story with someone close who could listen or read? If you don't feel safe sharing a story with someone, could you write a story in a journal or even post on social media? It can be healing when we reread something we have written and we are magically taken back to that moment. It brings healing to bring the thoughts out of your mind and memories in your heart are out in reality, no longer lost in the swirl of thoughts of all kinds inside your head. If you do post on social media, others that can relate or those who understand, will share a moment with you, supporting you in your pain of loss. By doing this you are validating your memories and emotions, you may be giving others permission to do the same if they are quietly hurting themselves from their loss.

A young kitten fell terribly sick and was with her person for a very short time. At just a few months old, she transitioned. The grief that followed was immense.

When her person reached out to me, the depth of her pain was very clear. One of the most healing steps she took, was to be honest- with herself and with those close to her- about how deeply she loved her little kitten and how much she was hurting.

She worried what others would think of her if she shared her grief. Quietly she had created a beautiful montage in memory of her kitten but it remained tucked away. After we spoke about the possibility that her honesty might also support others who were grieving quietly, she decided to share it.

The response was overwhelming. Messages of love and shared experience poured in. In allowing herself to express her grief, she realised she was not alone.

The animals know when we share stories and talk about them.

In an animal communication with a family, the mother of the family had lost her soul dog and she secretly reached out when her husband wasn't home. We connected with her dog, a gentle and loving golden retriever who loved her family very much. This precious being right away showed me a 7-year-old boy telling a story about her for his show and tell at school, he also had written a story about his beloved best friend. She really wanted her boy to share his story with the family. The mother said that yes, her son had mentioned his topic for show and tell as well as the story from school, but she wasn't sure what to do about it all, how to help him, when she was hurting so much and had left it alone. After talking about what could help them heal, her son was able to share it with the rest of the family. The beautiful dog in Spirit was so happy for them all and especially for her human boy that he could let out some of this love inside, come out by sharing. I received a message a few days later letting me know the family had listened to the son read the story after dinner one evening, it brought tears to them all but gave them all an opportunity to talk about their beloved dog. Once more in their hearts and memories, she was there with them.

Journalling

Journalling our way through the journey of grief can be so healing for ourselves. It can be healing to write for yourself, to allow yourself to acknowledge what you are really feeling. You can write to bring into the now, this moment, all the memories you are holding in your mind and heart. It can be a way of connecting with your animal.

It isn't looking into their eyes or feeling their fur in real life, I know. Once more, if I ask you to close your eyes for a moment and to think of your animal, can you feel their fur? Can you see their face? Can you remember every detail of them? Is there a memory popping up? Every loved one we have in Spirit, can be with us in the present moment. If you sit with intention with a journal, it can be a way to record what you remember or thought of in that moment. Just for you.

Your journal may be a place where you would like to let out your hurt, fears and frustrations. You may have big feelings about the events that happened leading up to your animal transitioning and don't know what to do with this. This could help.

The journal may not have the need to be beautiful or a keepsake, maybe this way of journalling is for messy writing and random thoughts. It could be a simple exercise book. It might be chucked out when you are either finished with the book or when you feel you have emptied all that sits inside your heart and head. Again, this will be your choice. My suggestion here though, is if this book is one of lower vibration, that it is not kept so you really do let go of the heaviness of it all when it is time.

When you choose a journal, consider the intention you have for this notebook.

If it is a process and you are doing this with intention to heal and remember, then choose a book that is beautiful to you and one you will enjoy writing in, do you like a bigger notebook? Spiral? Hard cover? Smaller notebook? Dots? Lines? Blank? What kind of pen do you love to write with? What will go into this book? Memories? Feelings? The journey of healing for yourself and checking in daily? Signs from your animal? Photos? Check in again with yourself, Is it for keeping? Is it only for as long as you feel it will be helpful? Do I need two notebooks?

What if this was a way you could keep your animal in Spirit as part of your daily routine while you heal? What if this could be a place for you to put your love?

Make the whole process easy so you do it. If it feels right for you, it could be one way you keep the connection, by you doing something in action. I know you think of your animal all the time, this is an intentional way to do something with those thoughts.

Memory Box

Having a place to keep items for your animal can bring a comfort to you. You may want to choose a special box. Make it a big enough box, if necessary, you can make it a place for you to place some photos, their leash, their blanket, favourite toy and their name tag. It is entirely up to you and my wish is that when you open this box, it only brings love to you. It may be with tears AND love and that is ok. Always love first.

For one dog Monty, his monkey stuffy toy was what he wanted to let his Mama know about in the communication. As I described his monkey, he was so excited! He showed me how gentle he was with it and how he slept with it at night. He loved this stuffy so much, it was his favourite toy ever! Monty knew his Mama had placed it in a box, along with his collar and she had a special place for it on the shelf of her bedside table. He also knew that just the day before, she had opened the box and taken a moment to look at the contents inside.

As a society we have rituals to bring completion to a person's life. We have ceremonies like wakes, funerals and celebrations of life. People come together, they talk, they share and it brings finality and closure that contributes to healing. With our animals we are often left with a gaping pain, no ceremony or closure. Most of the time, it is an urn we place somewhere and then what? What can be done to bring closure for our hearts? Until society catches up, you can create something for yourself to mark this closure that has meaning for you. For someone as special as your animal you get to choose what and how your heart will remember this moment.

As the animals have shown me, they want you to do what feels best for you, so you can be in a place of healing. For some, having a family gathering and sharing stories about their animal, brings healing with everyone having a chance to share. It may be visiting your favourite places to go with your animal and having a special moment there. It could be a special drink or activity in memory of your animal loved one.

Anything that brings meaning to you counts and it will be different for everyone. Talk about your animals, remember the funny things they did, share some special memories together. The animals love what you choose to do, even if it is a small gesture, they just want you healing and taking care of yourself.

In communications the animals have shown that they are with you through this process. They know what you do to remember them.

> *For one cat, she showed me a big lion statue in a backyard. I don't always understand what I see with the animals, but this felt important, so I shared it with her person. When I mentioned the lion statue, her person burst into tears as that is what she had placed in the backyard to remember her little lion. It was comforting for her to know her cat knew what she had done in memory of her.*
>
> *In another communication, a beautiful beagle in Spirit showed me a special plant that was his. It was a rose bush in a pot sitting on his front porch right where he used to sit. When I shared it with his Mom, she smiled a huge smile and explained that the roses were what she chose to remember her boy. Every time she looked at them, she would remember him sitting on the porch in the afternoons and it brought a smile to her heart. On the day that we connected with this beagle in Spirit, it just so happened that it was his anniversary day. Spirit always has perfect timing.*

In our family, I had a portrait of Gordon that I had painted when he was still living, this portrait brought so much healing for our family. To be able to look at this painting and see his eyes meant so much. I had it low on a side table at that time and my 5-year-old daughter kissed this canvas every day. A portrait has a unique aspect to it when it is painted from the hand of the artist. Capturing the soul of the animal through their eyes and feeling the love from them forever in the artwork is a gift that keeps giving. There are many pet portrait artists that can do this for you, do your homework and see who feels right to do this for you.

There are other keepsakes you can have in memory of your animal, a tattoo, a photograph, a paw print or piece of jewellery. What matters is that it isn't a case of just having the object but giving meaning to it as well. Take a moment to feel it and make it memorable.

For a cat in Spirit, he showed me a silver bracelet on his mom's nightstand, it was shiny and placed in a pouch. He said the bracelet was for him and his name. I saw an 'S' charm. When I asked about it, his Mum confirmed that this bracelet with a very special charm on it was a gift from her husband when her cat transitioned. The 'S' was for his name. It was given to acknowledge all the love and care she gave to her animal and the love they shared.

In another communication I was shown daisy chains.

This beautiful dog had been in Spirit for a few months and her Mum asked me to check in with her. When I connected with her, she showed me multiple daisy chains and said to me "She has daisies around her". When I shared this with her person, she explained that a funeral she had to attend just a few days before had daisies all around. She beamed as she then showed me her arm, there was a tattoo with a daisy chain, the daisy chain had been added especially to remember this special little girl.

Creating a Sacred Space for your animal and you.

Our lives are so very busy and everyday life can distract us to no end. It can hurt when we haven't taken the time for ourselves to stop or acknowledge how we are, let alone how we are feeling and healing. When thinking of the word altar, you may think of a sacred space. When you approach an altar in a church or place of meditation, there is a quietness as you look at the altar and the intention behind it can be felt. We are not intending to worship your animal either, more so, creating a place to remember them.

What if you could create this special space for you and your animal? It doesn't have to be a large space at all. It may be a little table or shelf. It could be a corner of a room. Or it can be as elaborate as you like as well. Your intention and the meaning you give this moment is what will matter the most. What would you like to feel when you look at or are in this space? If you decide to create this space, will it be a place you sit for a moment? Will you meditate here? Will you be standing for a visit? What will be more suitable for you and your life?

When you choose how this will fit into your day you can then decide on what kind of surface to place your items. If it is a moment, where you are standing, is it a shelf or a table? If you are sitting, is it a lower table or a space on the floor? Is there a cushion for you to sit or kneel on?

To lay a cloth or fabric, can be symbolic for setting the intention that placed on this cloth, is what I have chosen for myself and my animal, in remembering them and myself throughout my healing journey. It can be any fabric; it designates where you will place your chosen items.

Do you wish to light a candle and stay here for a little while? Is it a tealight? Candle? Scented? Do you have your favourite photo that you would like to place in a frame here? A photo with that perfect shot that brings a smile to your heart when you look at it? You may like to place some crystals here that you feel will help you in healing and place them lovingly on your cloth.

Do you have a special deck of cards where you can place one with intention to consider as you go about your day? Are they oracle cards? Affirmation cards? A quote that encourages you? What brings meaning to you with your animal? Have you found feathers since your animal transitioned? Do you love a special kind of flower? Maybe even a special stick you came across that your animal would have loved? It can be any item that evokes healing and love for you and your animal.

For one client her space for her and her animal was the surface of a hand carved foot stool, not a large space by any means, yet on this surface were items carefully chosen by her. Not everyone is understanding, yet, when it comes to acknowledging how much one can hurt when grieving. It can hurt so much to be told 'It's just a dog/horse/cat'. So much weight and love rests on that word 'just'. This client was not confident to set up a particular space where everyone could see. She did not want to be questioned about this space and why it was there.

Her altar was set up and taken down daily, the action of setting it up daily brought her comfort. It gave her the opportunity to stop and feel, as she chose from a selection of items to arrange to set up for a quiet moment. When she was finished for the day, all the items were placed carefully in a box ready for her to arrange again tomorrow. More than anything your animal wants you to feel good and peaceful. How ever your altar looks is for you only and not for anyone else to determine how it looks or criticise in any way. This is your space you are creating for yourself. Do you light incense in this space? Do you play music? Do you write in this place? For me personally, my way of ensuring healing and love is shown in all ways for myself and my animal during this time. I take the time to ask: Does it look good to me? Does it smell good? How does it make me feel?

I hope these suggestions can start you on a path towards creating your own sacred space. Your animal doesn't need you to do this, but they will be with you when you set the intention to spend a quiet moment with your heart.

Rituals

Could you come up with something to create a new ritual to remember your animal? In our family, we love Christmas. We remember Gordon at Christmas with special ornaments. When we see these ornaments, we share a funny story or memory of Gordy when he was with us at Christmas, like the time when he stole packages from under the tree when we went out. We came home to find them unwrapped but not touched. Gordon wasn't impressed with the contents and that memory always makes us smile.

For a birthday or a happy gotcha day, could you remember them by doing something special or going somewhere they loved to go to? A favourite park maybe? Could there be a favourite treat to have in memory of them?

Children and Loss

For children, the loss of an animal is their first experience of grief. Please be gentle and age appropriate in explaining the process of passing to your child. For ages between 3-5 years old, they may not be able to comprehend the concept of permanence yet, meaning they may think this is temporary somehow. It is important to be clear and with kindness. Refrain from using the term 'put to sleep' This can invoke fear and confusion about when they or any loved one goes to sleep. Please avoid saying "He went away". This can create confusion about separation. Instead, be clear and concise. Tell the truth gently. Be honest in your answers and keep it simple. Answer only what they ask. Explore a meaningful way to say goodbye with your child. There is a ceremony suggestion at the end of the book if you would like an example of one. Sometimes we don't have all the answers to our children's questions and that is totally ok. It's always appropriate to say to a child. I honestly don't know the answer to that, I wonder about that too. The question of what does dead mean, can come up and in this case again, it is important to be honest. A simple explanation can be the animal or persons body stopped working, they can no longer eat, move, make sounds or sleep. They have changed form and we keep all the love and memories we have of them. Allow your child the opportunity to talk about how they feel when they bring it up. Reassure your child that nothing your child said or did caused the passing of your animal. You can ask them questions such as 'What do you miss most about (insert name)? Talk about the memories of your animal, reminding them the love is always there for them from their animal. You can explore ways to express their emotions with creativity in making art, writing a story, writing a letter to their animal or creating a scrapbook of photos of them with their animal. Children can respond differently in their grief. They can seem totally fine one day and then ask questions or cry on another day. They can weave in and out of this so please be sure to check in regularly.

For our family when our cat Molly transitioned, my youngest daughter did not cry or seem to be affected. It took 3 years later for her to finally cry the tears inside. All along the way, we regularly talked about Molly and gave every opportunity for her to express herself and only then when she was ready, did she allow herself to cry and let it out. Children need to know that how they are feeling is normal. Please do all you can to validate them. Talk about their thoughts and give names to the emotions they are feeling. Give a safe space to express feelings. When you can name the feeling, you can give safe ways to express the emotions. Offer hugs, give time alone, giving suggestions for an outlet for anger, are all ways that can teach children how to express their emotions.

It is equally important to own your feelings and model how you process grief. You are allowed to cry; you are allowed to explain why you are feeling upset. In doing so, you are showing your child that feelings are real and teaching them how to manage them.

Although this is painful, the loss of an animal can teach children something profound. That love matters with the animals and that endings are a part of life but not the end of loving.

If handled gently, this first experience of loss can build empathy rather than fear. When you hold space for your children, you are not just helping them grieve, you are teaching them how to still love.

What about the next 'first'?

One thing for certain is that after your animal has transitioned, a first will come up. It could come sooner than later. You may ask how you will get through this? So many firsts show up. First birthday without them, happy gotcha day, Christmas, family gatherings or any other ritual you had with your animal there with you.

How do you get through this? Acknowledge firstly that this is one of those moments and it is a hard one for you. It is important to acknowledge this so you can do what you need to keep yourself calm and safe. You can cry and you can nurture yourself. Give yourself the space to not have to pretend to be ok or brave for anyone else. Could you do something nice for yourself also on this day?

Be kind to yourself and you are the one who decides what to do to take care of you while remembering them.

THE HEART OF THE MATTER

Love is felt by the heart and not thought by the head
– Rumi

When we experience loss and heartache, such as the journey through this grief over losing our beloved animal, our hearts are cracked wide open. Everything can hurt such as the words people say or what they don't say. We can feel an emptiness and lost when our animal is no longer there.

The pain can show up in a very real way with our heart literally hurting, it can honestly feel like someone has pulled a warm blanket right off you and now you are feeling raw, exposed and vulnerable.

If your heart feels broken, then we could also choose to see that the pain it has experienced, has created a crack of sorts and maybe this crack can open our hearts even more. We have previously discussed ways to be on the path of healing your heart and with good reason and now I get to share with you why.

Your heart is your connection with your animal. Your heart may be hurting at this time, a lot. It brings a whole focused awareness of our heart. It may have been experienced as silently existing up until now, it may have been you have experienced big love or big joy that you only really acknowledged your heart in those moments. Maybe you didn't feel anything at all for the longest time but now it is front and centre and it is hurting. It matters very much, this journey of healing your heart.

You were in close physical proximity with your animal. They were in physical form right with you. You used all your 5 physical senses with your animal smell, sound, visual, taste and touch. Communication happened between the both of you as you both perceived each other this way and sent messages back and forth to each other. They communicated with you with their sounds, with their expressions, their bodies, their movements. You communicated with your voice and your hands. You communicated love and committed with what you did for them. This communication brought an understanding between you both, however there is another way you are also connected.

You as a human being having this living experience, has a soul. You are an energetic being and your soul is the energy of you. An aspect of you remains in Spirit and another aspect comes to experience and create life here on Earth in the physical realm. You may have heard the term 'going home' and that is exactly the feeling the animals and people in Spirit give me when I connect with them.

We decide before we came here, what it is we will experience and learn while in our physical body here in this life. It would be like you sitting in your most comfortable clothing in your home, surrounded by all your favourite things, doing exactly what you want with the people you love. You decide that you want to go experience something somewhere else. Let's say you plan to meet up with family during a holiday trip overseas. You plan where you will meet up with them and how much time you will have together as well as what adventures or experiences you will have with them. You've decided now, your destination, your experiences and the people or beings you will encounter on your adventure away. You have a suitcase to take with you, it is relatively empty for now, just a few essentials, as you will buy things along the way. The time finally comes, it's this moment, you are on your way to experience your holiday! You get up, get ready and off you go! This is what I see our soul does when choosing the body or vehicle to go and experience this life. You won't remember everything from any other life experience, maybe remnants, much like your lightly packed suitcase. Along the way of your adventure of life, you are experiencing things and making memories, just as when you plan on buying things and having experiences along the way on a trip.

You will always have your home to go back to and be your comfortable self when you have finished that experience, it is how it is with your soul.

While you are here living and experiencing life, our heads are very much an important part of us as well, of course. We forget that the head is a servant of your heart. We are incredibly intelligent beings with our thinking minds and society revers this intelligence, however, the full breadth of being human is to acknowledge the heart and our emotions as well. It is using both as we move through this life. This is living in alignment.

Your heart is an important aspect that connects to your soul. Every living being has an energy about them. When a person is leaving their physical body, it is their soul that no longer is within the shell of their body. With the last breath their soul returns to Spirit.

So it is with the animals when they transition or change from physical form and into Spirit. Their soul is the part of them that continues to exist after transition, this is the part of you both that remains connected. You have heard the expressions 'Do it from your heart' 'Listen to your heart' 'Put your heart into it'.

Your heart is so much more than just a physical organ. Your heart has its very own intelligence and energy. You have an energetic field of energy that radiates from your heart. The intuitive heart is the part of you that is your first point of connection with another living being. Before you have time to analyse whether you feel safe with someone or even like them, you have already decided by your energetic response. Your intuitive heart has also been called your inner voice, your soul and your intuition. It is the place where thoughts and emotions exist. We can't see them with our physical eyes, they can't be measured or contained in any way, yet it is very real.

Too often, we are taught to disregard or discount what we sense from our heart. We give our permission for others outside of ourselves to know better about us than we do, even though it is our very own heart and our own feelings with its own wisdom and truth that knows what is best for us.

Our soul is wanting to experience this life in physical form. We have our heart that can give us access to the wisdom and guidance that is there for us to live our life according to fulfilling our soul's purpose. This includes relationships with people and the animals that come to experience life with us.

The way your animal experiences you is the energetic you, it is your heart energy that they connect with first every time. Imagine that there is a cord that connects you to your animal, it goes from one heart to the other. This cord you can't see with your eyes, you can't touch it and still it is very real. It is this heart connection that keeps you connected to loved ones, including the animals. This cord is one of love and it crosses all space and time.

This connection you have with your animal is the reason they know when to come lie with you, or you need some love from them. They know who they feel safe with always and who they want to be away from. It makes no difference to them what someone looks like, if they don't like someone they just don't. End of story. Energy cannot lie.

You are responsible for your own healing and happiness in general. No one else can do this for you. No one else can know the status of your heart. Only you. When we live life from the place of wisdom of our heart, we are living an authentic life. In our authenticity, we can trust what we receive from our intuition and to keep ourselves safe in all situations and circumstances as we go through our lives. The animals love this part of us first, all the other good things about ourselves come second, just as much appreciated always of course but you, the pure essence of you, is why they love you. Be aware of the energy you bring and of the energy you sense of another being.

SOUL DEEP

The deeper you go, the higher you rise

Your soul, that part of you that is pure energy, has a way to communicate with the physical part of you. It isn't separate from us but a part of who we are. It is the quietest and most important aspect of who we are as individuals and what makes each of us unique. It is the part of us that is an aspect of Spirit and has access to all wisdom and guidance.

Our soul wants to help us live our best lives, to follow our true path and purpose in this human experience. It is this part of you, that will be connecting with your animal's soul. When we live in alignment with our authenticity and soul, this is when we are living our best lives. We no longer come from a place of ego, the part of us that is about survival and has to have all the information and control over every aspect of life. Our ego is about protection and so can be based in fear. It is you against them. Competitiveness and control are the drives from a place of ego.

Knowing we have a soul and coming from a place of Spirit, we know we are a part of something bigger and there no longer exists you verses them. If Spirit or pure energy were an ocean, then our individual soul would be a droplet of water from this ocean. We come to experience life as our little droplet in individual form. An aspect of our soul comes to earth to experience a physical existence, and the remainder of the soul resides in Spirit. This is the part of us we can refer to as our higher selves. The part of us that can access all the wisdom and insight necessary for us to live our authentic lives.

When we return to Spirit, we are a part of the whole ocean of love once more, we return home. Coming from this place there is connection, community and working together, it is trusting that you are guided and moving through life in flow. Curiosity and wonder lead the way in moving forward when our soul's guidance is included.

There are ways that the soul can communicate with us, so our physical self can receive the information. Our soul language comes through our intention, intuition, imagination, emotion, inspiration and insight. All of this comes within. It is subtle and quiet and to be able to receive the information, we need to quieten our minds, go within and connect with ourselves on a soul level. How can we recognise when our soul is speaking to us and helping us live our best life while guiding us?

Intention

Your soul knows when you are following the path of what is meant for you. This is where we set a clear intention on what it is we want to create or experience. It is with a firm knowing that it will come to fruition knowing we are connected to source. This is not about acquisition of material things though that can be a part of the fun in it all. It is more about your heart's intentions. Intention is relevant to us with the animals in what we are expecting within our relationship to them. For you to connect with your animals it will come from your intention firstly. If you have the intention to be able to connect with ease, then so it is. If you wish to hear from your animal and it is your intention to receive signs clearly, then it will happen. The animals in Spirit know what our intentions are as do the animals that are living.

Intuition

Every human being has intuition. Intuition comes from you and is your direct connection with your authentic self. It is defined as the ability to understand something, without the need for conscious reasoning from physical senses. You may think that the use of your intuition or accessing insight and inner wisdom may belong to the mystics and those who you perceive as gifted. You also are naturally intuitive right now and have always been intuitive. Nothing else is necessary for your intuition to exist.

Intuitive information is coming through in your everyday life already, most often though, it is dismissed as random thoughts or just imagination. The information comes in a subtle way and not obviously. Being present in the moment of now and being aware of both the physical world and the nonphysical world, is how you can create more harmony in your life. In the physical world you can utilise all of your physical senses and for the nonphysical world you use your inner senses and feeling. You may think that to trust and use intuition means to not be realistic. Nothing could be further from the truth. Intuition is in addition to logic and complimentary. You could see logic as a head knowing, relying on what you have learnt and acquired in knowledge. Intuition is a deeper knowing from the heart and is wisdom from within.

What use is intuition if we don't use logic or reason in following through on what was given to us via our intuition? Intuition is not irrational or irrelevant to the rest of our senses. I see intuition as listening for your very own true yes or true no that is only for you to follow through on. You might recall when you had a bad feeling about something and went ahead and did the thing anyway, only to regret not listening to this feeling. You may also have followed a yes even when it made no sense at all to anyone else and the outcome was even better than you could have expected. Your intuition is quick and quiet. The information, or yes or no, will come through with no emotion. Your very own personal guidance system that is about trust and flow, will never flood you with fear when guiding you. It feels like a lighter feeling, following the direction of the yes or the idea that comes to you feels good. If it is a warning of some kind, the information will come in without emotion and calmly.

It is the first thought that comes as to what feels right for you. Have you noticed that we can feel all mixed up and confused when we start to analyse the thought? Intuition grows stronger when we honour and trust what we receive and what feels right and true for ourselves. Spirit can send us nudges to move this way in this direction, or to change direction if need be. You will find that when you are moving in the right direction and following guidance, everything flows to you. You are in flow and that is exactly the state we are meant to be in, living this life.

We experience synchronicities with the right circumstances and people showing up at exactly the right time. Our intuition can help us prepare for all sorts of situations and keep us safe when we need it. Does this mean we don't experience any hardship or challenges? Not at all. It does mean that you are guided through these times though. Intuition is taking the time to notice all the information around you and within you. You can receive the information much more easily, when you learn how it comes in and to be in a peaceful state to allow it to flow through. Learning how to use your intuition is what can help you accept there is another way of receiving information.

Following your intuition means to be honest with yourself. If something doesn't feel good or safe or right in any way, you listen and follow the guidance given. It means trusting what you receive, trusting that you are taken care of. It means to listen with your heart first, for what feels right and then with your head. Your head is the servant of your heart.

When you listen with your heart for what feels right or for what doesn't feel good, your body lets you know. You have heard the expression to listen to your gut. It is that feeling in your tummy that lets you know something isn't right. Another example is when you meet someone, and they say all the right things and come across as really nice but something just doesn't feel right? Your heart already knows by their signature energy feeling, if they resonate with you or not. Or if you are walking alone at night and the hairs on the back of your neck stand up? Or you shiver? These are ways that your intuition is guiding you to move closer to or move away from people, situations, circumstances and choices.

Letting your soul and Spirit be a part of your every day, means to be in a state of allowance and not having to control every aspect all the time. It means to allow changes as you go along, and your intuition will let you know when you need to make an adjustment or change. It means to be on the lookout for messages and meaning just for you, as you go through life. All kinds of information and guidance can be given, that you then feel your way to either a yes if it is meant for you, or a no.

Your soul deserves quiet time where you can listen and nurture this part of you. Incorporating quiet time in your busy life and finding a way that feels good for you to connect with yourself, helps to deepen this relationship with your authenticity and with Spirit. You are the expert on your life at any given time, you always know what is best for you and your opinion. What YOU think and feel, is more important than what anyone else thinks. It does not mean you don't listen or consider anyone else, just recognise and acknowledge when what you are listening to or reading isn't for you. When you begin to trust and follow through with your inner guidance and intuition, you are giving your authenticity the chance to shine, which is what your animals celebrate with you, being the very best you.

Imagination

'It's just your imagination' 'I might be crazy? Maybe I imagined it?' These are the kinds of comments people say when they have experienced something that was unexplainable or didn't make sense. This is when logic and reason come in. You try and understand but it still doesn't make sense, so then the experience is discounted or forgotten and put away in the back of your mind. It is easy to go straight to questioning 'Did I just make this up?' If you asked this question, then you may be jumping right to fantasy imagination. Imagination is what we use when we picture something or someone, when we remember and when we create. Children play with their imagination often and can create and entertain themselves for hours when given the freedom to do so. Artists and creators use their imagination when bringing creations to life and into form. You use your imagination when you are picturing something in your mind. If in this moment I was to ask you to think of an elephant with a purple flower, standing on a hot beach, can you picture that in your mind? Were you able to? Have you ever wondered where our imagination comes from? Have you ever thought about how it comes to us? Why did you imagine what you just did when you did? Of all the things you could have actively imagined in that moment such as when you daydream, something popped in completely unannounced.

Where does what you imagine come from? You have your subconscious mind, below consciousness, meaning you are not consciously aware of what goes on in this part of your mind. It is where you take in all the information, our brains can only process a certain amount of information consciously and everything else that we internalize, resides here in our subconscious. When we dream, meditate or imagine, we dip into this place.

Because our conscious mind is not in charge when we receive information through our subconscious, it can happen quickly and is quite often nonsensical. It isn't supposed to make sense which can make our analytical mind feel frustrated. This part of our thinking mind prefers predictability, order and being in control. The subconscious mind loves flow, play, creativity and ease. This is why our dreams feel like they make sense when we are experiencing them, yet to our intelligent minds, none of it really does.

Have you noticed when you daydream, you are in a relaxed state and for a moment, not right here in this moment. It isn't for a long period of time; it might even be for only a few moments and you were elsewhere? When we are in a state of allowing where you don't need to do anything or go anywhere, your imagination can come through. When you are in this state of allowing and not having to know an outcome in advance but are curious, this is when you are in the state of receiving information from your imagination. It is when we aren't trying to create anything with our imagination. When we aren't overanalysing or worrying, this is the head and heart space the animals in Spirit are able to get your attention. Society tends to refer to creative and constructive imagination most often. This is where creativity resides in all of its forms. We actively imagine creations into form. The imagination that requires allowing and receiving is the kind of imagination that intuition can communicate with us. It is the avenue the animals use to connect with you from their realm. You are not an active participant in this creating from your imagination. You are instead receiving imagination information.

A way to know if you are in the state of sending or receiving is to notice when you are pushing out an idea, that is sending out imagination, much like when I asked to visualise something. When you are receiving, your mind is not fixed on anything to do with whatever pops in at that moment.

We will explore the animals and you in detail a little later on, what I will say now is when you are open and curious with the attitude firstly that your imagination absolutely is valid and you are able to have the approach of 'I wonder', this way of being, is perfect for the animals to connect with you.

Emotions

Our soul has its own communication system through the heart, with our physical bodies and minds. This is through the language of emotions. This is a guidance system for us to know what feels true for us or what direction we need to go to live our authentic lives. Emotions are energy in motion. No emotion is good or bad, it is information that can be felt and transformed. Our thoughts can influence how we feel or how long it will be there for. Our soul will confirm when we are living our truth, by how we feel. The soul wants to feel good and be in flow so that we fulfil what we are here for in this human experience. When we experience feel good feelings and allow emotions to just be without judgement, it is living at a higher vibration. When we experience depression, anxiety, anger or sadness, these are lower vibrations. Notice I didn't say good or bad to be feeling any of these emotions. When we do feel the lower vibration emotions, it is up to us to acknowledge they are there, explore why, feel them and they can transform.

You may be asking in this moment, what is the difference between an emotion and a feeling. A feeling is created consciously by the thoughts we think about something.

An emotion is often present unconsciously, it is the raw reaction to an event and can be the basis of why we feel a certain way. An example may be that when you are a little person, you experienced sadness by how you were treated by other children at school. It hurt terribly and from then on, you have been very wary of meeting new people, maybe fearful, nervous or angry at the thought of ever being rejected like that again. The initial experience and emotion felt in that moment, is what is the basis of how you feel beneath the experience when you encounter anyone or any situation that is even remotely close to that. Another example could be, you have been hurt in love and so vowed to never fall in love or experience a close relationship again to avoid being hurt. The emotion could be rejection and you feel hopeless, vulnerable, angry, sad, used, upset and worthless.

It is important through this part of your journey, to be honest with yourself with how you feel at any given moment. It will allow you to learn about yourself in why you feel this way and what you can do to help yourself feel better. If you are feeling low or depressed, what can you start doing less or more of to start to feel better? The information is, better feelings means you are doing something right for you just as feeling worse is when you can ask, what needs to change? The underlying emotions that you are feeling when expressed, make room for better feelings.

If you feel you are unable to cry and feel numb, can you acknowledge what you are really feeling? Could it be guarded? Fear? Resentment, Anger? Sometimes when we acknowledge what emotions are there it can begin the process of releasing these emotions. You may notice you have been extra quiet and feeling tired. When you take the time to ask yourself what you are really feeling, it can be sadness or disappointment. Another example can be if you are snappy to those around you, or seem short fused and react to the smallest things in the biggest way. Perhaps what is festering under these reactions is frustration and resentment. It can be the emotion has been triggered by something in the present moment but has nothing to do with the present situation. Ask why you are feeling this way and what can be done to feel better? Do you need to check out for a moment? A hug maybe? Your heart has a much better chance to heal when you are honest with how you feel and give yourself permission to express the emotions that are suppressed inside.

Inspiration

I first came across the depth of this word Inspire when reading books by Dr Wayne Dyer. The basis of the word is latin In- Spire – to breathe into or move or Spirit. In - spire translates to In – spirit. Living in alignment with your spirit or soul.

When you feel inspired to do something, something moves you to do it. What inspired you? It is a question many a creative person is asked about their creation. Where did it come from? Their imagination. What moved them to create it? Their heart and their soul. Our soul sends us inspiration for ideas and creation. It guides us towards our fulfilment and life purpose. Our soul gives us nudges towards the situations and experiences our authentic selves want to experience. If we follow what inspires us, we then live in alignment with our soul. We then are in higher vibration because we feel good, just how the animals want us to be and they are our number one supporters in following what lights us up!

THE LANGUAGE OF THE HEART

The heart speaks in quiet knowing long before the mind begins to question.

If the part of us that is our soul, connects quietly with our heart region in our physical form, how can we recognise the language of our heart? How can we access our intuition or our inner wisdom? If our soul is able to guide us and we have this wisdom, how then you may ask, do we access this and what does it look or feel like?

You have this innate gift within you. It is a natural part of us as human beings. We may not have been encouraged to use it or even to recognise this part of ourselves. Some may have even tried to tell us it is wrong to try and do so and that anyone that can or does, is wrong. With this awareness on our hearts at this point of our journey, we can start connecting with our inner world and senses. I can assure you, most people, have had at least one unexplainable thing happen in their life.

They just knew something was going to happen and then it did. Some see something then it disappears, some have gut feelings that turn out to save their life. Others pick up a smell in the air or hear someone or something but no one or nothing is there.

It's all something, not nothing. You are about to learn about the ways in which we experience the information and learn the language of our heart.

Intuition is not a verbal language; it must be experienced to be understood and interpreted. It can make it difficult to describe what is experienced with intuition and make no logical sense. It is why when you try to explain a dream that was very real to you, it can make no sense at all to another person listening. It made sense to you in your experience as your subconscious mind was active in your sleep, yet when you engage your logic and then try to put words to it, it can sound like complete nonsense.

Just as we have our physical senses of sight, sound, touch, smell and taste, we also have our inner senses. These senses are known as the clairs. Clair is the French word for clear. When it comes from within, from your heart to you, you can't get any clearer.

As we explore each clair, I will give an example of someone with their animal in Spirit and you can get curious and explore which clair you feel is how you might best receive intuitive information.

It's not only one clair per person, we can all experience all clairs but most people will find they are more proficient in one or two clairs to begin with, more so than others. When you learn to receive information in this way, you will find you can become more fluent in each.

Introducing the Clairs.

Clair-audience

Clear – hearing

Clairaudience is the ability to connect to your intuition through inner hearing. With clairaudience information comes to you through hearing sounds, words, messages or music. You may be asking how this clairaudience may sound. It actually sounds very familiar, it's your internal voice, heard in your mind. You may think you don't have an inner voice yet we all do. How is it you remember your to do list for the day? When you tell yourself to call someone? Can you hear yourself telling yourself to do this? That is your inner voice. Or it can be when you recall a song you really like? Do you have one you can pull up in your mind now? Can you hear the melody? Can you hear the words? Are you listening? What are you listening with exactly? Your inner hearing.

Some indicators that you may be clairaudient could be you have a love for music, you notice sounds around you very clearly. You learn best through listening or prefer listening to an audiobook rather than reading. You may be very sensitive to sounds and loud noises. Another indication may be if you are a big thinker and, in your thoughts, alot. You may talk to yourself too. We all do it.

How do you receive clairaudient information?

In your own thoughts, in your own voice. Can you hear yourself reading this text right now? That is your inner voice. Did you just ask yourself if you could hear your own voice? What did it sound like when you asked? Again, that's you.

If clairaudience sounds like it's coming from you, you might think it could be difficult to know when it's from someone else let alone your animal. It makes sense that it would come from your own inner voice, that is familiar to you and your intuition never wants to create fear of any kind. When the information is coming from Spirit, it can happen as a random thought not related to anything that you were thinking about in that moment. You could be driving or doing dishes, you are thinking quietly but not stressed and the thoughts flow, when suddenly you think of your animal in the kitchen or how they used to do something in the kitchen. Guess what? That is your animal letting you know 'Hey I am here! Love you!'

You can hear it internally in your thoughts and it feels happy. Spirit will never bring any low vibe feelings with the thought. It's subtle and quick too, so it's a good thing to be mindful and present in any given moment.

Sounds

You may hear sounds, music or words in your mind. You may also hear sounds with your physical ears. Often the animals will show me them sending their people sounds to let them know they are doing just fine in their Spirit form.

An older dog in Spirit showed me him flipping a silver bowl at nighttime. He thought he was quite clever being able to do this. He used to do this when he was in his physical form when he would let his Mum know he was hungry. He wanted his Mum to know he was fine in Spirit, so he had done this a few times lately. When I asked his Mum if she had heard this sound, she was so happy because she had heard! She was so happy to know he had made this distinct sound, it was not just her wishful thinking.

A border collie female in Spirit showed me scratching at the back door and letting out a whine, giving me details of when she had been visiting. When I shared this with her people, they confirmed it happened at nighttime and were touched to know that what they thought they heard was actually from her.

Messages from your animals could come in the words of a song or in passing conversation that you happen to overhear when passing by. It could be the mention of their name or words meant just for you.

A handsome pit bull was in Spirit and I was talking with his Mama, who was really missing her boy. We were talking about him visiting her in dreams, it was her heart's desire but wasn't sure if he would. As we were talking, on my sonos sound system, the song 'Dream a little dream of me' came on. He was letting his Mama know he certainly would and he did show up in a dream just a few nights later.

A clever little girl dog in Spirit, had been sending her Mom a song. Her Mom said she had heard it at the strangest places, and it had happened about five or six times now. We confirmed this was from her. To prove it was her, she said she would send the song again, which she did just two weeks later.

Often the animals will scratch on the door as they used to when in physical form or their people can hear the clicking of nails on the floor.

The animals that would wear a bell on their collar when in body, have often let their people know they are around, by making the sound of their bell, a soft sound in the distance. It can be any sound that reminds you of your animal.

A neighbour's dog would whine softly when she wanted to come inside our house when visiting. We always knew it was her and would let her come in. A few months after she had transitioned, we again heard her distinct soft whine at the back door just as she had done when in body.

Listen with your inner ears, if you learn to hear and listen to your own inner voice and get to know what that sounds like, it will become easier to notice when the voice sounds or feels different to your own. You can practice listening with your physical ears by listening to a piece of music and noticing and focusing on only one instrument. The next time you listen to the same piece of music you can choose a different instrument to focus on.

Clair – Voyance

Clear- Seeing

Clairvoyance may cause you to think of the movie Sixth Sense and make you think 'I don't want to see dead people'. It seems Hollywood loves to use this clair to bring fear and drama to the screen. It isn't as dramatic as that and is more simple and subtle in its expression. Clairvoyance is not only for the psychics and mystics. You have this ability also. We are talking about inner vision, so having outer experiences with your physical eyes is not the common way to experience this, though it can happen. No you won't see anything scary either, unless you intend or expect to. I certainly don't experience anything that makes me feel fearful because it is not my intention in any way.

You may be clairvoyant if you are a visual person, you love to appreciate looking at beautiful art, or how something appeals to you visually. If someone asks you to picture something, you can do this with ease. If you can notice colours around someone or any living thing, you are using clairvoyance.

The information that comes via clairvoyance is through your mind's eye. It is the energy centre in the middle of your forehead. The pineal gland lies within our brains and is another avenue for receiving information. The mind's eye may give you sensations in the middle of your forehead such as tingles and you can differentiate between a feeling of pushing out or allowing in. When we push out, we are trying too hard and can feel disappointment and failure when we can't get anything. When we allow, there is flow and we let in what we are getting information wise. You use clairvoyance when you dream. Yes it's your imagination but using visuals to bring the information out. It can be like watching a movie in your head or having a mental image of something. If you have always had an active imagination or an imaginary friend when you were a child, you are using inner sight.

When receiving a visual via your third eye, you may see flashes of something or someone move in the corner of your eye. In fact, if you do think you see something with your physical eyes, it usually is from the side of your eye. Have you experienced that when you try to look at it directly, there is nothing there? When this happens, you catch a flash of something from the side of your eye, it is quite quick.

When the animals show up and pay a visit, many have shown me them in their homes. Your other animals in your family, may seem to be looking at nothing as they stare at a particular spot, or bark or make sounds at this space.

> *My sister was visiting me one morning and as she walked in, my dogs all sniffed her excitedly, this does not usually happen like this. Sylvie my Lhasa started sniffing the ground and growling as well as giving a strange bark. I checked it out and being a medium I sensed it was my sister's friend in Spirit visiting. I saw big black boots and where he was standing was where Sylvie was sniffing. I asked him to let the dogs know he is kind and a friend , which he did. I also explained it to Sylvie. She had a bit more of a sniff and then stopped completely. Now she knew who it was.*

Many people start to explain what they saw with 'You're going to think I am crazy.' Not at all. When I ask to share what their animal shows me, it then matches up to the same time and place that the person experienced this as well. For me in my experience when I am connecting with the animals, I utilise my mind's eye when sharing what the animals are showing me. It is only one of the 'clairs' that I use in my communications and it happens quickly. Most of the time it is within my mind what I receive, however I have seen the animals in Spirit with my physical eyes too.

I woke up to turn over on my side in my sleep one night, to find a brindle boxer dog looking right at me. In my sleepy state I complimented him how handsome he was and how big he was! I even let my husband know a boxer dog was on my side of the bed. I was sure we would find out in the morning who this boy was. Next morning I received a message that her dog had been in Spirit for a few weeks now and his Mom wanted to connect with him. She sent through the photo and there was the boxer I saw from the night before.

Clair- sentience

Clear – feeling

We are made of energy and have energetic bodies. In fact, it is energy that we all sense when we know we don't particularly like someone, or don't feel safe with someone. It is what you experience when you can feel tension in a room even in silence or what you sense when you visit a holy place or a place with denser heavier energy. With this clair, you can pick up someone's emotions and how they are feeling. It is the way an animal can sense if they like you or not, feel safe with you or not, gravitate towards you or move away. We as humans have this skill but are often taught to be nice and in doing so, ignore it. Every human being has a signature energy that is uniquely yours. Not everyone blends with each other either. That is our first point of safety in any given situation to know if we feel safe or not.

Remember in the introduction I asked you to take only what feels right for you while reading? It is using this sense. If you find you are often described as highly sensitive or too emotional you are sensitive to how an environment or people or animals feel. You may have a strong feeling to call someone and hear them say 'I am so glad to hear your voice! I was thinking how much I miss you!' You may have an off feeling when something doesn't feel right, a situation or a person. You may also sense happiness or excitement from someone well before they share with you any news to make them feel this way.

In relation to the animals, do you remember how your animal felt when they were with you in a room? Could you practice with your animals now that are living? Do you know when they are close by? Do you know when they have left a room? In communications, the animals show me when they have visited their people. It can feel like tingles. In body they have their body weight but in Spirit because there is no physical aspect, it may feel like a warm sensation or tingles.

A tabby cat in Spirit, showed me how he would put his paw gently on his Dad's face and watch him while he worked on the laptop late into the night. It didn't matter how late it became, he would stay as long as his Dad had his work to do. His paw touching was a distraction for his Dad to take a break. Now in Spirit, his Dad sat alone. I asked if he had felt a tingle on his cheek just the previous night. I described the room and he confirmed that yes that was where he was sitting at his laptop and yes he felt tingles on his cheek. He was so happy to know his cat was still with him.

Clair – Cognizance

Clear- Knowing

Have you ever just known something and you don't know how you know, you can't explain how you know either but you just do? Claircognizance is having a very strong clear knowing, this is your intuition. You may get messages that may seem out of nowhere. What can be interpreted as random is you experiencing claircognizance. It can also be experienced as just knowing how something will turn out. You may be the friend that everyone asks for your thoughts or opinion because you have a knowing. Experiencing this knowing can come to us through a strong whole body feeling. When we take the time to get to know ourselves and trust our intuition and the inner wisdom and guidance, this question of whether we should trust this knowing, is no longer even an option.

This is a good thing, especially when it comes to our animals in Spirit. Just because you can't explain it, doesn't make anything less valid. What matters most is that when you do receive a sign or suspect they have had some input of some kind or been around, you won't need to look for confirmation anywhere else or from anyone else. You will KNOW, like you know, that it happened. This is one way the animals send you nudges from Spirit.

If you have had a sick animal and you just knew something wasn't right, that is your intuition. Or maybe you had a knowing before choosing your animal that this was the one! I can't tell you how many times I have heard someone say 'I knew it!' in a communication. I am so happy to be able to give confirmation to them and I always hope it helps them trust themselves more.

The question to ask when you get this knowing is, does this feel true to me? By asking this, you can trust what feels true for you. This is your heart's confirmation when it is. When you ask is this right or wrong? This is analysing. This is asking from the mind first.

Clair-alience

Clear- smelling

Clairalience is when you pick up a scent in the air. Yet when you try to discover where the smell is coming from, you cannot find the source. It's a hello from those in Spirit. When you pick up a whiff of perfume or a certain fragrance of a flower or a meal, these scents can bring up memories and let you remember the person associated with these memories. This can happen with our animals as well. In communications with the animals, they will often let me know what their people had for dinner that they wish they had too. Lamb roast, meatballs, and barbecues just to name a few the animals have shared with me.

One Saturday morning as I sat at my dining table, I could smell a distinct horse smell. I got up and moved to the front of the house, no smell. I went to the back area of our home again, no smell. I sat back down and again there was the smell of a horse. I asked out loud 'Who is here that I can smell?' An image of a horse I know very well, in Spirit, came into my mind. I smiled and said hi. I could smell him standing near me for another five minutes and then it was gone.

Clair-gustance

Clear- tasting

This is when you can taste something that isn't there physically. It can happen as an awareness in your mind. If I ask you to remember tasting a lemon or a taste that you really dislike, you know what it tastes like. This is how it can happen when the animals send us flavours as well. It could be ice cream, you can literally taste ice cream, yet you haven't eaten any. This could be from your animal in Spirit that loved to eat ice cream, to let you know they are around. When communicating with the animals, this is the sense that helps me understand and interpret what the animals are trying to show me relating to food. For one special cat it was all about apples!

In a communication with a cat in Spirit from Italy, he gave me the taste in my mouth of the crunchiest, most sweetest apple. He was going to send this apple to his Mom as a sign of love from him. When I shared this with his Mom, she said she had no idea how this was going to happen, she didn't like apples and never had any at home as she didn't buy them. She thought it strange he would send this a sign.

A few months later, I received an email from the cat's Mom. She explained that she had gone out for dinner with a few friends at a pizzeria, she didn't feel like pizza, so she ordered the house salad, unaware of the contents she waited for her order. When the salad arrived, she took a mouthful and in the

Now you are aware of how important it is to take care of your heart and allow yourself to heal. You are also aware of the way we can receive information from our heart. All of this helps you remain connected to your animals in Spirit. Now let's turn to the animals and see how they have shared their experiences with me during their lives, in the dying process and transitioning to Spirit.

ANIMAL COMES FROM THE WORD ANIMA

Close your eyes so the heart can become your eyes and with that vision, look upon another world.
– Rumi

Who the animals are and what they experience

Animals are not human, though they do share aspects with humans. They feel, they hurt, they experience emotions. They are unique individuals as we are. They are conscious and aware as well as spiritual beings. We are beginning to realise there is a whole lot more to the world of animals than what we have been led to believe in the past. I bet you have known this already in your own personal relationships and experiences with the animals in your life.

Animals have intelligence. Humans try to measure the animal's intelligence through studies to determine how they think, problem solve and determine what they are capable of. However, the intelligence the animals excel in, is emotional intelligence, the capacity for sensitivity and to love unconditionally. Animals also have their spiritual nature and understand they are having a physical experience here with us. Animal comes from the word Anima. The Latin origin of this word is Breath, Spirit or Soul. To breathe life into, means to animate. I feel this word embodies the recognition and reverence I hold for the Spiritual aspect of the animals in every way. Yes, your dog that digs in garden beds and can be a goofball is a soul first. Your cat who can be a diva, is at the core of her a soul being. It is the same with every kind of animal.

The physical aspect of an animal is the physical form they have chosen to experience life here on the earth. This is their vehicle to experience life, and they know it is not for always. The emotional aspect of animals has thankfully now become much more of a focus for humans when interacting with animals. We have a long way to go yet but it is a good start in science, recognising the animals are indeed sentient beings. They have their own emotions, perspectives and feelings about themselves and their everyday lives with their people.

At a soul level, the animals have an acceptance and an understanding of life. They know they have their own purpose to fulfill here on earth and see the transition made back to energetic form, as natural and part of the ongoing cycle of existence.

They do not have negative beliefs or negative associations with the end of life as humans do. When connecting with the soul aspect of an animal in communications, they offer a different and meaningful view of their life with their person or people. Remember what you learnt about the heart and soul aspect of you? So it is with the animals also. At this level, the animals hold this incredible wisdom and contribute to our heart's and soul's well-being so quietly and profoundly in their physical existence and it continues when they transition. In tribal societies across the world, there is a knowing of the rhythm of life.

These people live in closeness to nature and have a strong awareness to the cycles of nature. An awareness of the continuation of the Spirit exists within these communities and cultures. When it comes time to farewell a loved one, it comes with an acceptance and even celebrated, as they know their loved one continues to exist in a different form. When we are not aware of this continuation of the soul's existence or the spiritual nature of animals or humans, this loss seems so final.

Becoming aware of the spiritual nature of animals offers a whole new way of seeing their leaving, as well as their existence. They have a purpose and intention of when the time is right for their transition to take place and preparation happens in the meantime. Not only are the animals preparing themselves, they are preparing their people and consider their people in their departure also.

How the animals experience the journey home.

The animals each have their own unique journeys home. Did you know that the animals have already planned for how and when they will go? Let's talk about you for a second. You as a soul has decided when to come to this earth and what lessons you are here to learn. You have also decided what it is you want to experience in this lifetime, along with whom you will have experiences with. Animals, also having a soul, they too, decide when they will arrive and who they will have experiences with. They know their purpose and lessons they are here for. I want to be clear on this because taking that into consideration, we can look at the topic of euthanasia.

Regarding euthanasia, it is never a good feeling to have to make that decision. For many people, the questions arise often, is it the right time? Am I being selfish in wanting to wait a little while longer? Am I wrong for not considering spending more money on treatments even though my financial situation is tight? Does my animal hate me for doing this? How can I ever forgive myself? I don't know your personal situation or circumstance in how your animal transitioned. I do know from all the animal communications I have had, that the animal already having decided how and when they will go, are not hating you for anything at any time. They have nothing to forgive you for. Your animal sees your heart and your intentions first and foremost and they know when you are choosing or deciding something out of love for them. The choices and decisions that you made, all have meaning, though it may not be apparent in that moment or around this time, you may have learnt something or feel you would have changed something or done something differently. You may have immense gratitude that you could help your animal peacefully in transitioning. You may also have a deep peace knowing you did the right thing, you trusted yourself in making that decision for your animal.

For some animals, the journey is long to transitioning, gently and slowly stepping with you on the path towards home. There is a slow progression of dis- ease in the body or a slowing down. It can happen over a few years in time. The appointments to the vet may become more frequent, the animal may need special care and treatment, the person has the time to become used to the idea of their animal's fragility and are right with the animal during the whole process.

The animals have shown me there is a purpose for the journey to be long for their people. It isn't an easy journey I know. It can be very painful to experience this, I acknowledge that as well. From the animal's perspective, it was for a reason each time. Along the way of this journey home with your animal, you may be learning about alternative healing therapies and through the treatments, you discover a love for a particular modality. There may be certain people you meet on your journey with your animal that are all a part of your purpose and plan in being here. Or you could become well educated with nutrition having to explore the solutions for your animal in the process. It could be that you wish to work with rescue animals more moving forward. At times discovering your next step in life includes this journey, in this way. It can be the next step is lit up for you to follow when you are ready. You could discover your voice and ability to speak up when needed for your animal and now are able to do this better in every area of your life.

The animals have often showed me how their person changed in this experience, they became much softer, their heart opened even more. There is a preciousness and an appreciation for the animal in a whole new way. No longer invincible or forever young, we realise they age physically and what they once were able to do is no longer. Time comes to the forefront as life goes on and, in this awareness, we come to terms with the gift that time really is. They also show me their people's strength and patience, the love that they give their animals, commitment of time and all the things they are willing to do for them. Our empathy can grow, our intuition can become stronger, helping us make decisions and choices and bringing an awareness when our animal doesn't seem right. We have an awareness of our animal, even more so, in this vulnerable stage and we do all we can to protect them and honour them in the process.

The animals know when their people need time to process and accept the fact of the animal no longer physically being there. They consider who their person is and what they need to come to that place of acceptance. The animals have shown me the gift it is, when you and your animal are in what I call the Golden age stage. It is as if a bubble has surrounded you, your loved ones and your animal, as you go through this time. Time here slows right down. Every moment counts and is precious.

Distractions from what is important may fall away during this time. Newfound joys in the little things and the quiet moments can be discovered through this time. For me, Gordon knew it would take me a very long time, I could cry at the mention or thought of him no longer being with me. I had a 2-year span from his initial diagnoses to the final moment. In that time, I changed a lot. It also gave me the time necessary, to help my daughters accept what was happening and for them to grow even more tenderness for the animals during the remaining time we had with Gordon.

Other animals have shown me the purpose of having their process happen quickly. Again, I acknowledge, this can be the most jarring and difficult thing to accept. Many people question why it had to happen the way it did and could they have done anything differently.

The animals have an awareness of how it could have played out if it were prolonged, as they know you as a person. They have an awareness of how their people could experience even more stress or feelings of helplessness than what they already had. Animals have shown me a soul awareness of their time to go, they already know.

A dachshund was the love of his people's lives. He went with them everywhere and had such a close bond with the three people in his home. His people were a young couple who had welcomed him home as a puppy. They had a roommate who they shared an apartment with and she loved this boy as well.

He was an intelligent being and listened very well. He was a sheer delight in their lives and to everyone that met him. One day while playing at the park, completely out of character, at the age of four years old, he ran onto the road instantly being impacted by a car. Devastated by the events and with serious injuries from the accident, they lovingly said goodbye to their boy. His people could not understand at all what had happened and why he would have done such a thing. When I connected with him in Spirit, he was so happy to know his people were checking on him and that they knew it was him sending them signs. After more 'conversation' between the both of us, I asked him what had caused him to run out on the road as he did.

He explained on a physical level he was distracted by something shiny. I was shown what could have been a bright reflection of some sort, perhaps the light hitting a mirror, in the general direction of the road. He ran towards it and it happened all very quickly.

His soul wisdom came through and he explained that he had fulfilled what he had come to do. His people were practicing being responsible together as a couple, raising and helping him learn and making memories together. He was especially proud of them both for calling each other Mum and Dad, for it was all in preparation for the baby that was on the way.

He had given me the news that his Mum would be pregnant in the next few months and that the baby would be a girl. Without sharing these details to his people, I didn't feel it was my place to share in case pregnancy wasn't part of their awareness yet. I implied that he had been the catalyst for a big change on the way. A year later, I received an email complete with photos of them both with a happy baby girl.

You may ask why it all ended the way it did, for some it is very traumatic and this is also why it is important to be gentle with yourself in your healing. I know for some, what is seen at that time, cannot be unseen. I would like to explain what the animals have shown me from their perspective.

The animals can sleep a lot in the last few weeks and during the final days before leaving. This is the time where they visit the realms of where they will go. I have found they play with their loved ones in Spirit and prepare themselves.

In my communications, I have also found, the animals practise being out of their physical body while they sleep. I sense that as time goes on, there is an emptying energetically. There remains a silver cord that keeps the connection to their physical body, so they always return. It takes a big surge of energy for the soul to separate entirely from the physical body. If the animal is wanting to be alone when they leave their bodies, it can be out of love for you to not have to witness the effort or bodily functions that can happen when the soul is leaving the body. We already feel helpless enough when we know what is happening. Please just know that it is out of love when they go on their own.

As they experience their final moments, the animals show me watching themselves from above their physical bodies. It is the same when there has been an accident, I am shown their perspective from out of their physical bodies. For some, the animals show me their consciousness coming back in the body and then being out again. This is confirmed by their people when I hear them say 'She was there for a moment but then she wasn't'.

Molly at 19 years of age was found at the backdoor of the laundry lying in the sun at 5.30am. This was her eternity day. She had eaten dinner the night before as she said she would and was discovered exactly where she had said she wanted to be in her final moments. My husband brought her into me in the bedroom and we wrapped her up, I held her and checked for any sign of life, there was none. No breath, no movement and her body was stiff. We laid her in her bed and waited for the rest of the family to wake up so they could say their goodbyes. Two hours later, as we lifted her up from her bed, we laid her on the table, we all were gathered around her. There was an energetic shift I felt, I saw Molly's leg move! I was so shocked, the next thing, she moved her head and opened her eyes to look at the girls once more. She made eye contact with everyone as we all said our words to her. As I was holding her driving to the vet to assist her, she wrapped her paws around my arm and hugged me tight. I let her know I accept this and love her so very much. I could feel her drifting in and out of her body. As we assisted her in transitioning. I did not feel her in her body but watching us from the corner of the room.

When the animal's soul leaves the body, the body will continue to do its own thing while the life force exits. This can cause twitching, jolting, sounds and excretion. This is the physical aspect of the animal closing down. The animals show me them watching their physical bodies, they have described at times, the room and who was there with them, along with what was said to them in their final moments. All they show me is from a view above their physical selves. The animals often have their loved ones coming to welcome them home and are waiting for them. I have seen when other animals in Spirit are around the living animal. They are so excited while they wait. Just be aware that if your home feels full of animals when you are at this time with your animal, you can be assured they are waiting for your animal!

Two Dobermans, a male and female were together for such a long time and the female was so sad when her brother returned to Spirit. When I was connecting to her, she was days away from transitioning. I explained what she was showing me in the communication. There she was on a soft blanket on what looked like a bed, it was her mattress on the floor. As she lay there, right next to her was her brother and he was so excited!! He said that his mum and dad had photos in white frames hanging up, of both of them together and he wanted his family to know that he would be with his sister. I was shown the exact photo I had been showed, there it was hanging on the wall!

If you are considering at this moment, the animals that have been surrendered and in rescues, then please know that they too, are welcomed into Spirit with so much love. I have been shown the biggest feeling of safety and love. It feels like VIP treatment for these precious beings. It is rest and love and healing on the agenda for the next part in time.

I hurt for those animals that don't have any human that knows them and loves them, only those who are there with them in their final moments. I had to connect with a dog that had just gone through this experience.

Dusty was a pit bull in the US. A young badly behaved male by human standards, he was now deemed as dangerous, as no one had taken the time to train him or socialise him. No one was there to give him the time he needed to learn and so he was to be euthanised. I connected with him on behalf of someone who knew him and had done all she could to help him before his departure. I asked him if he knew what was happening to which he answered yes. We had a big connection and I cried during this communication. He had been let down by people again and again and it was not his fault. He lived in fear and it was expressed as aggression. I apologised to him again and again.

At this moment, when I connected with his soul self, he had no anger or resentment towards people. He even told me he planned on returning and gave me the details, (which it was confirmed a few months later). I kept thinking of Dusty and made a point to connect with him after he had transitioned to see how he was. When I connected a few weeks later, as I tuned in, he bounded to me happily, to let me know he was ok! He showed me what he had experienced when he transitioned. I had tears in my eyes as he showed me a big Angel cradling this boy in their arms. He was held with so much love and protection as the Angel walked into the Spirit realm with him.

No one ever goes alone. Not people and not animals. My heart knows this, I hope your heart can feel the truth of this too. Everyone has a guardian angel with them all through their life. We are never alone and I am so very relieved and happy to know that the animals are embraced in love as well.

But I think my animal is fine now and it's not time yet....

Perhaps you have had an animal that has been weak, sleeping a lot, not really interested in food at all. You made the call and all has been set for the appointment. A short time later, there is your animal asking for food! They are back to their usual selves, and you now question if you made the right decision. This is a surge of energy the animal is experiencing, the one purpose of this is to enable the soul of the animal to separate from the body. I have found that when the animals go through this and you witness it, it is for your heart to remember them as energetic and their healthy self and not as the sick, weak, injured or tired being their physical self has become.

The other way the animals can experience this surge of energy is at the latter stage of their transitioning. It could show up as the animal fighting the Euthanasia or in the actual shutting down process, this surge of energy is the last push of sorts to separate the soul from the body. Not every animal needs to experience this either. It is the same with how people transition, some go very peacefully and others it takes a lot of time or the body still continues on because of this energy surge, even though the soul may be ready.

The Heart Snapshot

In communications with the animals, I have been shown what has been described to me as the snapshot of the heart that the animals take with them in Spirit. It is like a forever photograph. It can be at a favourite location, or with their people. You can recognise this precious moment when in their final days you will see them take in what they are looking at and scan very slowly or take a long look at a face or in your eyes. Your heart will feel it and know if it is when they look at you. If they don't look at your face as their last snapshot, just know you are in there too. I have witnessed so many beautiful moments that the animals have taken these heart snapshots, the people have always confirmed this moment and recognised it.

For one German Shepherd gentleman, he requested one more visit to his favourite park. He found walking very difficult with the arthritis in his hips but wanted his parents to know that he wanted to sit with them once more at the pond with the ducks. His parents made the effort that weekend after the communication to go to his favourite park. They brought a picnic blanket and carried him to lay and take in the view. He showed me his happiness when sharing this moment with me. He took in the faces of his loving mum and dad in that moment, the smell of the park, the sound of the trees rustling and watching the ducks bobbing on the water in front of him. His heart was full in that moment.

In another communication, it was time for a precious girl to transition.

A sassy french bull dog was ready to go but not without instructions for her family first. I was shown a beach where she loved to run and play on the shoreline when she was younger. They hadn't taken her here in a while. Her special day, by request, would be a visit to this beach and finished off with some hot chips. The family did as she asked and they made it a memorable day for the whole family. I had explained what to look out for when and if she was taking a photo with her heart to take with her in her final days. They managed to capture her in that moment at the beach. She scanned the beach very slowly, as she stood in the water taking it all in. She turned around to look at the family, another long look, in that moment, the family also snapped a photo of her that is with them for always.

In a communication with a little silky terrier in New York, she showed me her heart snapshot was in her final days looking up at her Mama as she was held in her arms gently dancing together in the bedroom. She shared this precious moment with me that no one else knew about to give to her Mom, so her Mom knew it was from her and very special to her too.

Why couldn't I be there with them when it was time?

This is a question I hear often. People do all they can for their animal and every kindness and thought for your animal is appreciated by them. They know you are doing everything out of love. I know how much you wish you could be there with them; it is heartbreaking for us when they pass on their own. Many animals who did leave on their own have shared this with me. Some prefer to only have the animals with them when they go. The other animals offer support or comfort by just being there. There are no added emotions, and they go quietly. When it is their time to go, some animals wish to go on their own and let the body do what it needs to do without any interference. They also don't like to perpetuate more feelings of helplessness for you than you already feel. Again, the last surge of energy takes a lot of effort, and they want space, to be left alone while they go through this last process. Whoever is there when they go, is meant to be there. Sometimes it can be they want to have the human that helps them be strong and feel safe to usher them into the next form. Animals have shown me how strong human's love can be that if they are present, separating from the physical form can be even more difficult.

They already know.

The animals can let their people know who they want to see before leaving this earth, for some animals it can be they request to see the young children around them before they go or grandparents. Or it could be other people they love. They can also let you know if they would prefer to be assisted or not, to transition at home or at the vets.

For a male Afghan in South Africa, he requested to transition at home on his blanket with his favourite toys around him. His people did as he asked, setting everything up as requested. When it was time, he waited quietly on his blanket for his family to gather around.

For another cat, she did not wish to transition at home. Her wish was to be at the vet clinic, as her person was very sensitive to the memories made in her home and felt that there would be too much sadness. Her person had tears knowing her animal knew her so well.

For another dog she wished to transition in the backseat of her car, so many drives had been enjoyed from there. She requested her Mom hold her in the backseat. No longer able to use her back legs, her Mom lovingly took care to make the backseat as comfortable as possible, she had soft music to play as well, as she was also preparing for the moment. Their vet was so co-operative and accommodated for this dame to transition in the way she had wanted.

When I have asked how it feels to leave their body, the animals have described it to me like this.

An older female labrador, was in so much pain from her arthritis, her ability to walk was very limited and it hurt so much to try. When I asked her to show me how it feels to be in her physical body, she showed me how heavy it felt and what an effort it was to move herself. I was given the feeling of the heaviest coat you can imagine on the hottest day. Extremely uncomfortable. It could only be doable if you don't move at all in this coat. This is what she showed me. I was sad for her and knew her people were doing all they could to help her be comfortable and she let me know it would be time to go very soon. There she was then in Spirit when I connected with her again and the lightness I felt from her was so free. Her energy was so big! She showed me her movement and her ability to run again, sheer excitement and joy was what she was feeling.

The animals show me when they have assistance via euthanasia, they may show fear. This can be because it is the vet's office and that may not be their favourite place at all. They may be frightened because there has been no explanation from you, or they can feel all that you are feeling. It could be they can pick up on your dread and they don't know exactly why.

Perhaps they may want you to be holding them or on a certain blanket or have their favourite toy with them. It is these details that aren't acknowledged that can bring fear into the experience. It may also be your fear they can sense, picking up on your energy they can become anxious, so it is so important and helpful for you to come to a place of peace when it comes time to assist your animal.

The animals are not afraid of transitioning though, it is a natural next step for them. They show me how it feels when the liquid from the injections flow in their system and they have shown me the final time they close their physical eyes.

That isn't it, that is not the end.

The very next blink, it is their soul eyes that are still open. If an animal has been watching from above, it is the view from those eyes, from here on, that they show me. They show me quite often, coming to where you stand or are with them in their final moments and trying to comfort you to let you know they are ok. Everyone including your other animals want to know your animal is ok.

Here is a communication with a beautiful horse as he experienced his transition.

A beautiful male horse, lay on the floor in the barn, gently closing his eyes as he felt the relaxing feeling flood through his body. All went quiet after hearing his Mom's voice whisper in his ear her final words. The final breath exhaled as he found himself lifting out of his body. He looked at his horse body lying there surrounded by his loved ones. No more heaviness and tiredness, he felt as light as air in this form!

He walked over to where his Mom bent over him crying. He stood quietly next to her, sending her all the love he possibly could, he was so grateful for the life she had helped him live despite all his limitations. He wanted more than anything to comfort her and to lean his head on her and be close to her without a physical body, how could he do this? With intrigue he decided to find out what he could actually do in this way of being. As a horse that suffered with heaves, (for you who don't know heaves is like an asthma condition in horses) he could never run with the other horses for as long as they did or as fast without having to stop and catch his breath. It was an effort to breathe after a big energy burst and an even bigger effort to accept that he couldn't do what the other horses do.

He promised himself that when he had the opportunity to leave this body, he would firstly run in the paddock as fast as he possibly could. He would do this to prove to himself that he could do this without any struggle or having to stop to catch his breath. He would do this multiple times and felt excited when he thought of how free it would feel for him!

He would stand in the house that he longed to be inside of, just to experience it and stand next to his Mom in the kitchen. He was so excited to be doing this and to finally know how it smells inside, what the sounds really sound like of laughter and busyness from the children and how it all feels! Now had come the perfect opportunity!

But firstly, he ran in the paddock with freedom and pure happiness to be able to feel the lightness and ease as he ran beside another horse, around the paddock he galloped, a few times, as he said he would.

Finally, after all that time looking up at the house that he would watch, through the crack in his stall, he finally made his way inside. He walked through, taking it all in and there in the kitchen stood his Mom at the sink having a quiet moment to herself. He stood behind her, having a good look around, taking note of the sliced bright green apple to the left of the sink. He loved her so very much and hoped she knew just how close he was to her at this moment. To let her know it was him, he focused on her little finger and made it twitch several times. He hoped that she would notice.

When I conveyed to his Mum what he had shared with me, she said that one of the other horses was running around the paddock multiple times after this being had transitioned. It made her so very happy that her boy was able to do this after seeing him suffer with his heaves through his life. It was also confirmed that she had been in the kitchen that evening and yes there was a slice cut from the apple she was eating, on the side of the sink, just as I had been shown. When I mentioned her little pinky finger twitching, she was so excited to know that her beautiful horse had made it twitch!

The other animals in your family.

The other animals have an awareness on a soul level that their sibling is going. I have been shown the other animals sitting silently together, exchanging communication between each other. There is an exchange between the animal leaving and the other animals concerning what changes are coming and I have been shown in communications, little details that were given to another animal family member in taking care of the people.

> *A beautiful brindle rescue dog was preparing to transition, her people were not exactly sure how much time they had left with her. They did all they could to ensure she was always happy and comfortable. When I connected with her, she showed me her taking the time to give some instructions to another dog within her family. This boy was her little brother and he really looked up to this girl. She loved to snuggle up to her Dad at nighttime before sleeping. She would get cozy in the crook of his arm as part of the night time ritual. She had instructed her little brother to do this for their Dad when she was in Spirit. After she had transitioned, I connected with her and she was so happy because what she had asked for, was being followed through. I asked Mom and Dad if they had noticed that their boy dog was giving cuddles, just like their girl had done, to which they happily said yes to.*

Each animal within your home has a purpose with you and each animal loves to have a job to do while living life with you. When an animal has a job, they feel as though they are purposeful. When one of the animals' transitions into Spirit, there is a shuffling and reorganisation for who does what and if it is a single animal, they need time to work out what this loss means to them. The animals grieve like we do.

They miss their family member and for some, it can feel very uneasy for a while. The animals also have a sensitivity to the energy or feel of your home and they are concerned for you too. If you are crying, they want you to know they are there. Let them know you are ok even if you are crying and that you are all going to be alright. Keep the routine you have as close to normal as possible as this helps in predictability for your animal. Sometimes our routine is the only thing that can bring a sense of some kind of normality while we go through our mourning.

On a soul level, the animals know what happens when one of their family has transitioned to Spirit. On a physical level, there may be confusion and feelings of sadness and fear. If you have had your animal assisted at the vet, please ensure you let your animals know where their family member is and what happened.

If you have them assisted at your home with euthanasia or they transitioned on their own, if your animal is asking, please allow your animals to say their goodbyes and see their family member. It brings a closure for them also.

> *For one husky, there was constant crying and howling since his older brother had transitioned and was now in Spirit. His Mom contacted me to see what could be done to help her boy settle. The whole family was sad about the loss and a feeling of emptiness was evident. When I connected, he showed me his sadness, deep sighing, not eating. Wanting constant cuddles*

from his Mom was an absolute necessity to try and feel somehow ok.

As we got further into the communication, I asked him to share with me his relationship with his brother and to share some memories. It made him happy to share with me his pain and his memories and the love they shared. He was very worried about the whereabouts of his brother. He thought they were just going out and he would come home. His brother had let him know he was going but he had no idea it was that particular day. He waited and waited for him to come home. Only he never did.

He showed me his confusion that all of his brother's things were packed away and the warm body he would lie next to at night, was no longer there. He missed his brother painfully. He was also very worried about the sadness the family around him were feeling, as well as the responsibility he now had as the only dog. He wasn't sure if he could take on what his brother used to do in the household. It was a big job. I reassured him that everyone was healing and that all would be ok. No one was expecting anything from him and only wanted to help him. I explained what had happened with his brother and asked what could help him soothe his pain. He asked for his brother's blanket to sleep with as it was packed away and he longed for his brother's scent to fall asleep with. His Mom gave him the blanket and had a conversation about their brother and that he was so loved and all would be ok. For the first time that night, this boy had a good meal and with a full belly, he laid on his blanket and slept deeply.

For another cat, I was asked to communicate with him as he had become really nasty with his cat brother and out of sorts, not affectionate at all with this people, after the passing of his dog sister. Everybody was so very sad. He was heartbroken and didn't fully understand what had happened when she didn't come back from the vet's. Everyone rushed out so quickly that day and then he never saw his dog sister again. When asking him what was going on, he explained his sadness and frustration and just missed her so very much. I asked what could help him, he asked where her bed was now. It was in the back of the van and had been left there. He requested for it to be returned so he could smell her once more. His people brought the bed back inside as requested and very tenderly, this cat walked up to the bed and sniffed gently, he then laid himself on her bed and curled up and slept. He returned back to his usual self, asking for pats and attention with his people and had patience with his cat brother once more.

When the time is right for the animal, they can see their animal family member in Spirit and they can communicate with each other. You can recognise this when you see your living animal looking at an area as if someone is there, which there is of course. Your animal in Spirit is visiting and they can see. They may make a space on the sofa where they used to lie with their loved one, you may have your animal in Spirit sitting with you in that moment. Or perhaps your animal wants to stay in the area that your animal in Spirit would spend alot of time. This may be a place your animal in Spirit returns to when they come for a visit.

Animals grieve because the physical aspect of their loved one is no longer with them. They grieve for this loss and changes it means for their lives now. The animals check in to see how you are feeling and can be uneasy if all at home is not right. I am not suggesting hiding your pain, not that you can anyway with the animals. Be honest as always with how you feel. Lots of cuddles and slowing down time is all helpful in healing, not only for the animals but for the humans as well. Talk to the animals, let them know what is happening and where their family members are. Through the communications with the animals, another sacred aspect in their leaving, is in their assistance to their people in handling grief. Often it is not just the loss of this precious animal. When we are feeling vulnerable during this time, any other grief from losses of both animals and people past can come to the forefront. As much as you may have thought it was done and gone, it has come up again so you can really heal that part of you hurting from then as well. Often, if we haven't felt safe to feel how we feel with the loss of an animal previously, we now have a chance to acknowledge all that is sitting there from then too. Pain is pain, so being honest with how it can feel compounded, can give you the space and time to heal what needs to be healed and acknowledged. It can be at times, that this part of your animal's journey in their loss, is part of their purpose in being with you.

A LIFE OF PURPOSE WITH YOU

Love is the substance of all life. Everything is connected with love, absolutely everything
– Julia Cameron

When I connect with an animal, I am shown who you are as a person. Not what you do for a living or where you live. Not how wealthy you are or the face that you show to the world. I see you as your animal sees you. The animals know exactly who you truly are. You know this already because who you are when you are at home by yourself, is the very true you.

Have you noticed how some people turn into a big kid when they play with the animals? The way they talk to them and the big smiles they have on their faces is a huge indicator that the most precious part of that person is loving interacting with that animal.

I have the honour of the animals showing me their person's authenticity. If you feel as though you may have lost this part of yourself-the authentic you- you can rediscover it by acknowledging your heart and listening to your inner guidance. It is the part of you that knew what you liked and didn't like when you were little, before anyone made you think or feel that any part of you, was wrong.

If you have a toddler in your life, watch them for a moment and see how unapologetically they are themselves. That is who I see when the animals show me you.

The animals show me often how soft hearted and sensitive their person is. Every time I mention this sensitivity to a client, I will often be told not to tell anyone, along with a giggle. The person they show to the world does not always include this part of them but your animal sees and knows.

They know when you are smiling with your heart, the animals have come to let me know this is called a true smile from the inside. This is what I have been shown and what I use as a term to describe a heart smile. They know when people don't smile true. The animals always know the true feelings or intentions behind the words and faces of a person, which can be why perhaps you can perceive someone as nice and yet the animal won't go near them.

The love that you share with your animal is one of the purest loves you will ever share with another being. They have learnt how to love us and are our best supporters in remembering who we really are. We also love our animals so very much, yet we are still learning how to love others anyway, without any kind of conditions attached.

The animals know when you are experiencing pain quietly, whether this be emotionally or physically, maybe you don't let anyone else know how you are hurting but your animal cares very much. They show concern for you, by tending to you or overseeing you while you rest.

They truly observe what goes on and have their own perspective about events and situations.

> *As I was driving my car, I heard a voice pop in. A dog I had communicated with a few days before, let me know it was him. This boy loves his Mama and is always close by her as they live their best lives in the Mediterranean. He was very concerned about his Mom; he brought me an awareness to her chest on the left-hand side. He asked me to check in with her to see if she is ok because she was crying and breathing funny according to him. I was concerned and thought of what to do next.*
>
> *I messaged his Mom; to let her know I had heard from her boy. I didn't want to impose or alarm her and shared with her what I had been shown and what he had said. She was laughing when I told her this, which I was thankful for. She then explained, he was showing me her doing a breathing technique to move grief from her heart. The previous night, he was sitting next to her mat, watching as she was doing this exercise. Ah, now I understood! I asked her to please let him know she was ok when doing this technique, which she did. He was thankful his Mom was ok and to know what she was doing.*

They say hindsight is a wonderful thing. When we reflect, we can make sense of things that have happened or how we felt about something. For you to reflect on your animal and their life with you, you can begin by remembering how your animal came to be with you. Some ways the animals come to be in our lives, seems to be magical. It felt just right or the way you discovered the animal or how you rescued this animal. Yes, you were a big part of their healing but that animal was also meant to come to be with you for your healing and play an important part of your life. You also have come into the animal's life to assist them fulfill their life purpose. For some people, the bond experienced with an animal is unexplainable but so very obvious. The relationship experienced together reveals in time the why.

Animals have different purposes when they come to live their physical experiences. It may be how your animal came to be with you seemed random, when really, it was all part of the plan to come to you.

The pathway to fulfil their purpose with you means that the timing and events leading up to that moment where you both meet is perfect. From a soul's perspective, no matter how adverse life was being experienced for you or your animal, it is in perfect timing and comes about in the perfect way. If you look back and think of even two weeks before the time your animal came to be with you, it would not have been the right time or life was too busy. If your animal is a rescue and had other people in their lives before coming to you, there is a purpose for that to have been part of your animal's life as well.

We have established that we are more than just our physical selves, as are our animals. We are spiritual beings having a human experience. Your soul has its own purpose here in this physicality and you have most probably had more than one life here on Earth. We have soul groups that tend to have the same souls as we travel through our lives and in each different lifetime, the same souls play different roles to learn and grow to fulfill their individual soul purpose. It can be why you can meet a person and feel as though you already know them. Families tend to be in the same soul groups, your brother could have been your grandfather in another life or even an Aunt just as an example. Learning about past lives is fascinating as you can discover who was who and when in your past and to discover your soul's purpose and lessons of different lifetimes. The animals, are also a part of this soul group that you are in. The animals can also have had a past life with you. It could be the last past life or a few lifetimes ago. It may be a reason why your soul can recognise this being. Your animal could have been another animal as well in another life, your dog in this life with you could have been a horse in another life with you, in another part of the world.

The animals' soul has a purpose as well as mentioned before. All living beings are learning and growing each lifetime.

This is where you come in and the importance and relevance of you coming into the animals' lives. Your personality and who you are, along with your life circumstances and the people you have around you, are all perfect for your animal to heal and learn from you too. This has all been agreed on a soul level before you both came into physical form, to fulfil the soul's journey and learning on this physical plane.

You may have a family with children or live with other people, when your animal comes to be with you and is living life with you. Your animal has a unique relationship with each individual and plays a different role in that individual's life. Everyone who is there at that time is meant to be there. It may seem like less than perfect, the life circumstances we find ourselves in, yet all is exactly as it is for the fulfilment of your animal's soul purpose and yours. You both coming across each other is at the perfect time, every time.

We all can agree with the fact that forever is never long enough for the love we share with our animals. We wish it was for always and always. Time for the soul of any living being is not relevant. We know the animals don't read the clock. Yes, they know your routine and will certainly let you know when it's feeding time. It isn't by linear time though. That is a construct the humans came up with. The animals follow the rhythm of the day.

For the animals, some stay their whole life with one person or family. Another animal may only stay for a very short time with a person or family, on their way to where they need to be next. The lessons they have learnt or experiences they have are part of their journey in their personal life. Animals play different roles at different times with different people. Or it can be different roles at different times with the same person or people.

A beautiful tabby cat named Bella showed me the perfection of when she arrived at her forever home she is now in. At the time she showed up at this particular home, she was heavily pregnant and looking for a safe place to birth her kittens. She was undernourished and very frightened but knew the place she had found was safe. When I shared this with her person, she had tears.

At the time Bella was found, her person had lost all hope and had fallen into a deep depression after losing her mother with whom she had a very close relationship with. Unable to sleep or eat, life was difficult and the days went by aimlessly. When

Bella came at just the right time for her to give birth to her kittens but on a soul level, she came to be a healer for her person. It is often that when I connect with the animals, so many of them have come at the perfect time when their person or a person within the family is going through a hard time of some nature. It could be recovering from a loss or an illness and there comes this precious animal that gives them unconditional love and purpose. For some, their animal is the only reason their heart is still open just a crack and they can give and receive love. It could be that too many people have hurt this person, and an animal is the only living being they trust to love and be loved by.

The roles the animals play in our lives.

To my understanding, there are different roles the animals play in our lives with us and at various times. The roles they play, can vary in each personal relationship they have with humans. It can be the animals have fulfilled all roles at some point in their lifetime with you. These are examples that I share and in no way are limited to just these roles. They are intertwined and changeable always, this is to help you recognise a point of reference so you can recognise how your animal's role played out in their physical life.

Healer

Often, the animals come and be with a person or in a family as a healer. Healing may be happening for the people in the family after a loss of another animal. They can be a healer for a hurting heart. The animals can come to ease loneliness or to help their person feel loved when they have lost faith in humanity or believe they don't have the capability to love and be vulnerable with another person ever again. Being the source of unconditional love that the animals can be, brings healing. Knowing someone is waiting for you and wants to love you can be the most soothing balm for you. Perhaps welcoming another animal into the family is what is healing, in recognising you can love again, when you thought you could never love again at all.

Cats are very often clever in knowing just where to send their healing energy. They may sit on the person or draw attention to a particular area of the body. If you are anxious, the simple act of responding to your cat asking for scratches or to be picked up may just be your animal picking up on how you are feeling. When you hear that purr or feel the softness of their fur, all stress can rest for that moment. Sometimes the train of thought bringing more worry, can be interrupted as you focus on your animal.

For one ginger cat, he knew very clearly just what his people needed for healing and made sure they knew it too. His Mum had developed a neurological condition that was affecting her eyesight. While her medical team were trying to find out the cause, she was resting up as instructed by her doctor. He stayed with her. One day she had decided she felt well enough to get up out of bed, this cat did not agree. Every time she tried to get up, he would push her back down and meow loudly in protest. When she had contacted me about this, I asked him what the reason was behind this behaviour and he explained his reasoning. He was worried she would fall. It became clear to his Mum he was insisting she needed more rest and she understood why. When it was explained that more movement was going to happen and it was safe, he let his Mama get up from bed. He also sits on his Dad's chest whenever he is unwell with a cough or a flu, sending his healing as he sits on him. He also sits on Dad in the mornings to help him start his day slowly and with intention.

Here is a communication with a cat whose purpose was to help heal a grieving heart from a previous loss.

I was contacted by a mama of a young cat in Spirit. She was hurting deeply over the illness and sudden loss. The kitten had only been sixteen weeks old when she transitioned, it felt to her person as though life had been cut heartbreakingly short.

When I connected with the kitten, she showed me what had happened for her to decline so quickly. What hurt her person the most, was not being about to hold or touch her again as she regressed in health.

During the communication it became clear that this loss was touching something much older.

Another woman in Spirit came forward. I recognised her as a close Aunt to the person. The relationship had been very strong, yet there was an unresolved sadness around the Aunt's final moments. Once again, there had been no opportunity to properly say goodbye. No chance to hug her, no space to express any love.

The kittens' transition had mirrored the Aunt's passing in a subtle but significant way. The emotions that had been there for years rose to the surface in this new grief.

The message from Spirit was gentle and clear, the healing needed now was not only for the loss of the kitten but for the earlier loss that had never been fully grieved.

It was an honour to witness the shift that followed. Layers of pain were acknowledged and healed. Both the kitten and the Aunt were grateful and relieved for the person that the weight that had been carried for so long was finally understood and released.

A sassy and cheeky cocker spaniel showed me how hard hearted her Dad was. She was the light of his life as he had been hurt in relationships and didn't trust people so much. She was one of the few living beings he loved. With her, he melted and did all he could to ensure his little girl was happy. She was so grateful and was very happy to be a part of her Dad's journey. By her being in his life, she had kept his heart open to receiving love and took care of it with all she had, loving him unconditionally through her years. She knew her purpose was to help him heal and prepare to love another person again.

When I connected with her in Spirit, she was happily jumping around for her Dad had met a woman whom he had been in a relationship for a few months. She really liked this person and could see how good this was going to be for them both. She also was happy that the woman had a little silky terrier with her who really liked her Dad too.

Teacher

How frustrated could you be at times during your animal's life with them? It's ok. It happens. Don't stop there though, how have you changed in your approach or interactions with your animal, or how has going through their aging process or illness changed you as a person? Would you agree that you may have grown more patient or compassionate? What about more sensitive? What did you learn in helping your animal while you were helping them in their lives? Often people will discover on reflection, that because of their animal, they came across an alternative therapy that they love and want to learn. Or they have become involved in a rescue or group that is right where they need to be.

For one dog Shar-pei, her skin condition was incredibly raw. Her digestive system was suffering, and her person was so unsure how she was truly feeling. Even though her physical discomfort was evident, This girl still had a very happy disposition. Being a Shar-pei, trying to soothe her skin was proving to be a huge challenge. When I was contacted, we asked for her input on how she was feeling. She was happy natured for sure and showed me her determination to be happy, despite what was going on with her skin. She gave us her input on what was helpful for her and her person listened and explored more on what was given in the communication. On her journey she came across canine nutrition and gut health and this sparked a love to learn all about it. For the remainder of her dog's life, her Mom implemented all she learnt and her dog's skin and digestive system improved dramatically. During her learning, she also pursued formal learning and gained qualifications in being able to help other people with their animals through nutrition and supplements for gut health. Without this beautiful girl, this may not have happened.

I connect often with a stunning gelding; he is one of the most gentleman- like personalities I have ever come across. He is a handsome horse with a strong yet gentle presence. When I was contacted by his person, I was honoured to have met them both. We explored what we could about this being, his likes and dislikes and views on various things about his new life at the ranch. This brought much more understanding between them both. I was so happy because he let me know that he was going to be a great teacher for his person. He showed me his patient nature and gentle way with her. This was the very first horse she had ever had and had wanted since childhood. She was in for so much fun and a beautiful relationship as she learnt all she needed in her horsemanship. Through the communications I've been shown again and again, his clear communication, his patience and love he has for his human. Each time, I get to see how much she is paying attention to him. She is learning so much in her riding and experiences with this gentleman. They get closer and closer and truly are a team.

Catalyst for change

This can be the most difficult role to see at the time of the animal's life. For me personally, Gordon was my catalyst. It was a huge loss that catapulted me onto my path to discovering my life's calling. For my daughters, going through the grief of losing Gordon, helped them learn how to look for signs from Gordy and to accept more easily and go through the loss of Molly our cat, a few years later.

For others it has been what has happened afterwards, that has given insight as to why the animal was in the person's life or left when they did. As people are loved by their animals and are encouraged to move more or become involved in different activities involving their dogs, they often are put in the direction of where their inner being wants to go. For some, it can be after the loss of an animal that a move to a new location, house or travel can happen. For others it can be the welcoming in for a new animal that is meant to be with you on this part of your journey on Earth and you are a part of their plan as well. It can also be the welcoming of another little human being, a baby.

> *On a routine visit to the vet, I looked up and saw her dog in a photo frame. I heard her immediately say 'I am no longer here. It was time to go. I am so happy and free! She is having a baby, it's a girl and arriving in September. It's my time to go so she can have the time to be with her baby.' I didn't say anything to my vet when I walked in and when I asked how she was she told me how her sweet girl had passed and how sad she was. I listened as she shared with me what had happened. The next part of the conversation was all about discovering her*

pregnancy and that they found out it was a girl, and she is due in September!

A big tabby cat had transitioned a few weeks prior to the communication I had with him. His Mom wanted to see how he was, so we checked in on this lovable tubby guy. He was so happy when I connected and showed me, he had been around his mum in just the last few days as I explained what he was showing me. She had just purchased her tickets for her to go travelling around Europe and wanted to know if she had his blessing. She felt strange to not have to care for him and there were so many empty quiet moments now. She felt it was the right time to go and do what she had always wanted to do. He was so very happy for her and knew this is what she had been wanting to do, her commitment to his health as he went through kidney disease stopped her from going anywhere. Until now. He wanted to let her know that he had left so she could go. He said the time was right for him to go. On her travels she found a special someone who is her partner now and she knows her beloved cat is happy for her.

Guide

Your animal is a very wise being. They are always cheering you on and loving you for who you are, so you can learn to trust yourself and become more of your authentic self in your life. They are encouraging you always to head in the direction of your purpose and true way of being on this earth. It can be that they guide you from their physical existence and they can also guide you from Spirit. Now when I say guides, I don't mean with matters of the human experience as you may find with other kinds of guides. When I say guide, it can be that they guide you for growth emotionally while in relationship with the animal. They can guide you career wise, steering you that way, due to issues or circumstances of their life with you. They can guide you from Spirit when it is time to choose another animal and send you signs to nudge you in the direction your heart wants to go. When you reflect on how you have changed since the arrival of your animal and all you have learnt in your everyday simply by having an animal, you may discover just how much of a guide your animal truly was to you during their life time. I honestly see every animal as a guide in how to be loyal and to love unconditionally. I know you can recognise this in your animal too.

Protector or Guardian

We see ourselves as the animal's guardian or parent; it is true that we are. You also are being protected and taken care of by your animal. When we have been hurt by other people, we may have believed that we would never love again and then arrives this being that totally makes a home in our hearts and here we are again, loving someone. This is for your healing. If you have depression and feel hopeless about the future, then comes a bouncy being or animal that needs love and to feel safe just as much as you do. This happened for the both of you.

They guard your heart first and foremost. They know when you don't feel safe with people, they know when you are sensitive, and the happenings of the day have hurt you. They know when you are crying on the inside or wracked with worry or fear. They do all they can, to let you know they are there and that you are loved. Your well-being is their main concern always. No, their life is not just about you but this is an important part of helping to ensure them that their environment is one of safety. This is because the animals are sensitive to how you feel as the energy that you bring wherever you are, has a feel to it. It can feel safe, light, warm and loving or it can feel dark, heavy and sharp. Sometimes the animals will do what they can to change this energy. It is why they pestered you to go for a walk when they did. Sure, it's routine, that is only one aspect, the other is that it is for you, so you go outside and disperse stress or worry, one step at a time while you walk. Maybe their behaviour at times, was to bring attention to them instead of focusing on what is causing overthinking and overwhelm in your life at that time. Other times, it may be that you are reminded when it is their feeding time or they ask if they can go with you to the park that you take them to, as you head to your car. The act of following a routine can bring a feeling of security and safety to you as well as your animal. Everyone feels safer when they know what happens next in their daily life.

HAPPILY HERE AFTER

*We didn't realise we were making memories, we just knew
we were having fun*
– Winnie the Pooh.

When it was time for me to let Gordon go and for his little body to be taken away, I was left asking, what happens now? Where is his soul going? Will I hear from him again? Is he alone? Where is 'there' anyway? Is he going to be ok? Maybe these are questions that you have also asked after you have said goodbye to a loved animal. I will do my best to answer from my perspective, again, I am not an expert because I am not in Spirit. I only have the honour of seeing glimpses when I connect with the animals and meet the people with them, though it isn't every time that a person is with the animal. It can often be other animals with your animal.

I have the strongest feeling though, that as we experience our lives here on earth, we all have our own unique perspective. You and I could even be together in the same scenario or situation and you could have an entirely different way of seeing it all than how I see or experienced it. I guess the best way is to explain what it is I do and then translate to you what I experience with the people that allow me to connect with their animals in Spirit.

Firstly to understand where 'there' actually is, let's discuss all things energy and vibration. It may sound like overused New Agey words when I say these words but stay with me and let us explore what this means and how this is relevant for you and your animal.

The animals are at a much higher frequency than us as humans. Their physical aspects are already giving evidence of this. For example, the animals have supersonic hearing and their noses are able to pick up the slightest of scents. They can tune into us as humans with their ability to sense how we are feeling or what our intentions are without us saying a thing. Every animal knows a fake smile or pretence a mile away and they know when they are safe and when they are not. The animals have mastered the ability to live in the present moment. They do not spend much time at all in the past as we can do as humans, nor do they worry about the future. If you take a moment to reflect on what you think about, how much of it is in the past or the future? The animals are very much here and now and they know how to live life to the full in this moment.

The animals when living, don't tend to stay in place for long where they are feeling lower vibration emotions around them either. You may have noticed that if there was tension or an argument in your home, your animals disappear? They do not enjoy this kind of energy and so remove themselves. You are not being judged by your animal for how you express your feelings or for how you are feeling. No emotion is wrong or bad, it is information for us as to what we are feeling and why. We have to acknowledge the not so good feelings in order to allow the better feelings to exist and bubble up to the surface. This is why I have said in previous chapters to be honest with how you are really feeling and to give yourself the permission to feel it. The lower vibration feelings and emotions that we as humans experience are, worry, jealousy, anger, fear, depression, sadness and anxiety to name a few. The higher vibration feelings and emotions are gratitude, love, compassion, happiness, peace and joy again, these are the lighter and better emotions we can feel.

We never experience only one emotion. If we really pay attention there are a few different feelings swirling inside. You can choose which emotion or feeling you want to focus on. The more you acknowledge what you are really feeling, the easier it becomes to choose how you are wanting to feel in any given moment. I am not being all love and light either here. We have the not so good feelings and emotion to guide us to what we don't want to be feeling and we can choose to do or behave in a different way that can create the better feelings. It doesn't make the not so good feelings go away, it is giving the space for you to feel it all and letting in the better feelings along the way.

The density of our material and natural world in solid form lowers our vibration also. When the animals return to Spirit, they are at an even higher vibration just as we are when we are in Spirit. In this vibration, we can't see our animals in solid form or feel their touch as we did when they were in body. We are able to catch a glimpse in our peripheral vision, the side of your eye, this is where the eye captures more light. Have you noticed, the second you try to look straight at what you thought you saw, it is gone? This is one reason so many people think they saw something but can't be sure.

Now if Spirit is a higher vibration, we experience this in a different way than how we experience our 3D reality. I will explain how I understand the Spirit world being here and not anywhere else and again, you feel if this is true for you.

I am now going to ask you to use your imagination. Imagine a book. This book represents your intention to connect with your animal. It is a book about you and your animal. When you open it, inside are beautiful images of the two of you together. It's personal and sacred. As you read this book, you are choosing to only focus on your animal. If you have fear about opening yourself to anything else in the Spirit world, you don't need to worry. Your intention is clear. This book is about your animal and your connection. Nothing more.

Now imagine that at the front of this book there is a transparent sleeve- a clear overlay that can be placed over any page.

This transparent sheet also carries images.

You turn to one of the pages and place the transparent sheet over it. Suddenly, there is more detail. The image feels richer.

When you lift the transparent sleeve away, your original page remains exactly as it was. Nothing has been taken away from it.

The transparent sleeve represents Spirit.

Your physical life- your memories, your love, your experience with your animal are already beautiful on their own. But when you understand

Spirit and include your soul in the experience, life gains another layer of meaning.

Spirit does not replace your physical connection. It doesn't take anything away. It adds depth.

Living your life with the intention of including your intuition and living from your heart, is like placing the transparent sleeve gently over the page. The transparent sheet is the realm of where the animals are. This is how the animals are right here with us, not on the original page any longer but the additional magical realm that is transparent unless we pay attention. When we include our heart and our intuition, we begin to notice it and we realise they have been right here all along.

We all have our own unique experiences and perspectives about life here on Earth. Someone living in one part of the world, can have an entirely different way of experiencing the world than how you experience it. Differences in location, culture, religion, personality and the way of interpreting experiences, all contributes to the individual meanings given to life. The same is with the animals here on Earth. As I have connected with the animals that have transitioned, I have learnt that it is the same in Spirit for the animals also. I strongly sense that in Spirit, it is a unique experience for all of us. Sure, there are similarities in what people have experienced in Near Death Experiences (NDE) as they share their stories. Just as we have nature around us or water, what you experience could be entirely different to how I experience it. I could describe what I experienced with water from the ocean and say 'The water at the reef today, was crystal clear and a peaceful turqouise colour, I could see right to the very bottom of the ocean floor.' You might say, 'I saw the waves today and they were so big and choppy as they were hitting the shoreline on my walk at the beach, this morning.' Both are true of the water in the ocean and both very different experiences.

I say this because when I connect with the animals in Spirit, I could have one dog showing me a village in Costa Rica and as I describe it the person will verify, it is a place that this person can recognise. I will see a golden glow in the light to signify to me that it is in Spirit and not a memory here on Earth. Again, I am only explaining my experience and how I am shown where they are in animal communications. For another animal, a cat for example, she may show me a living room with the most luxurious comfortable chair. Both are relevant and real to the animal.

To give you another example:

> I connected with a beautiful female puma, who was a rescue and could not be released back into the wild. When I connected with her and she showed me where she was in Spirit, I saw an amazing waterfall and high rocky mountains where she was bounding and playing with another male puma. Both stopped for a minute on a rock up high, to take in the breathtaking view. I described this scene to my client. I also described the other puma I saw with her, his personality and how he was connected to her. It was confirmed that this was her best friend who had transitioned two years prior. It was also explained how sad she was when her best friend had transitioned. The sheer happiness that these two expressed in the

communication, was so obvious. I felt it all and it brought a tear to my eye that they are reunited once more.

The animals often show me other animals they are with in Spirit and these animals can come from the person's childhood or be the animals with other family members or friends in Spirit. It is always so intriguing to me because you never know what the animal will show you or who they will have with them when I connect. I have to clarify though, that just because I am shown them in this scenario with these people or animals, it does not necessarily mean I will see them again in that scenario in another communication. It is very similar to a call made on a mobile phone to a particular number at that time and they pick up in that location.

For a little dachshund, I was asked to connect with her in Spirit. In the first communication, she showed me her in a kitchen with the most amazing smell of freshly baked cookies made by an older woman who loved being in the kitchen cooking and baking. This woman had her other dachshund there also. Both dogs were running and playing in this kitchen and there was a message of love for my client from this woman, her German grandmother, who was well known for her delicious fresh cookies when she was living. When I connected another time, as I am seeing where this little girl is, I see her by a lake and running on a beach. This time I see darker skinned people of African origin and I see a scene where there are a group of people sitting together and eating and laughing. There she is sitting next to a gentleman and listening to everyone laugh and talk together. I am slightly confused as this is nothing like I saw as before in the previous conversation. I have to trust what I am seeing and shared what I saw with the client. We had a giggle as she then explained these were her husband's family members and identified and clarified who it was I had described to her.

Because Spirit is a higher vibration, the density and physical form is not necessary in Spirit. When the animals do show me their physical self, they will show me the physical version of themselves when they were in their prime. If not in this form, they will show me themselves in a way that can help their humans know it is them. I have to smile sometimes because the animals are so very excited to have their people ask about them. When I am in their awareness, they can show me as a ball of colour first and then show me their physical form. It is the same for the people that are there in that moment. They wish to send a message to the human and to reassure the person, that they are with their animal. I ask them to show me something that the person could recognise as them. People that are part of the soul group can come through too in a communication and it can be at times, that the person may not have known them in their lifetime, yet there is always a reason as to why that person has come through at that time though, I usually am informed about the why after the communication. When people come through, there is always a message of love for the person, from the person in Spirit. I get curious each time I am connecting and when I am having a 'look' around the animal to see who they are with at that moment. There are always others around them and I wait to see who comes forward in that particular communication.

In a communication with a Pomeranian dog, he showed me how he was in Spirit as well as who he was with in Spirit. It meant so much to his Mom to know that he was with her

Sometimes if we are missing a human loved one in Spirit, when they come through, they can share memories that bring back the love for a moment! Sometimes it can be the reassurance that they are with your animal that can help in healing.

Many people question what happens if they move house or location, can their animal find them? My answer is a very big yes! The love that you share with your animal crosses all space and time. It doesn't matter where you are or when, they know where you are and can reach you. Your love is like an internal navigation tool. You can move multiple times and the animals know exactly where you are and can be right there. Remember, they are still here, just in a different form and in a different realm.

Now is as good a time as any to discuss the Rainbow Bridge. It has comforted us as we picture our animals in a magical place where there is a bridge that they cross when they go to Spirit. We can imagine them sitting there and waiting for us for the day when we will meet them there. There are some aspects that are true of the Rainbow Bridge. Yes there is a bridge of connection that exists between you and your animal so there is a 'bridge'. There is also a 'crossing over' of sorts to being in another realm and form. I know that losing your animals is already hard enough and all we want to know is that we will see them again and that they are safe and happy where they are. I would like to suggest something even better than a place where your animal is waiting. Again, if you don't feel it is true for you, leave this right where it is. I don't mind at all, I just don't want anyone thinking that their animal is ever dead and gone.

A glimpse that I have had is when it is time for you to arrive home in Spirit, a memo of sorts goes out to your soul group who are all together in that moment, this includes the animals. Travel is just a thought away, so they think of you and there they are all together! The call has been made, that you are on your way and when you arrive, you are welcomed by all who love you in Spirit, so you can be sure that your animals are there too!

If your animal has a unique experience of the Spirit world, then you can be sure that what they are experiencing for themselves is way more fun and exciting than sitting in one location and waiting. What is even better is because the Spirit world is actually here with us, albeit in a different realm, being beside you or visiting you is only a thought away also. Often when the animals have transitioned, they will show me visiting their home in the next few days. They have shown me sitting in the backseat of the family car and jumping on the bed that very night. They are checking the other animals in their family and checking on you. They discover how easy it actually is and how amazing it is, that they can come be with you in a thought and that quickly.

The animals are aware of what you are doing while they are in Spirit. As we discussed before, the animals want you to be happy with what you have chosen to remember them by. They show me what you have done so I can share with you that they know and love what you have chosen. They also show me moments that they have been present while you are living your everyday life.

In a communication, a golden retriever in Spirit showed me sitting on a backseat and drooling. Next to him on the left-hand side of the backseat was his gruff older golden retriever brother. I saw a dark blue colour around the brother's neck, someone was reaching behind from the front seat and holding an ice cream for him. The look of disbelief was comical. When I described this to my client, it was confirmed they had gotten the brother a happy gotcha day ice cream. He was wearing a dark blue bandana. It was Dad who was holding the ice cream for him and this had happened just a few days ago. Both Mom and Dad knew how much their boy in Spirit would have loved an ice cream too in that moment. He totally knew all about it!

In another communication the first image I was shown by a staffy, was a fluffy lion. It was her most favourite toy and she loved it so much. She was showing me where her Mum had put this lion. I saw it on the bedhead in the bedroom. When I let the client know, she confirmed that this was her most loved toy even though she had a big basket full of toys. As I described what I had been shown, it was my client's bedroom and there on the bedhead was the little lion.

A cheeky fox terrier in Spirit asked me to ask his Mum my client, to please bring home the grey blanket. He showed me how much he loved this blanket and that his Mum had been

One theory that exists which saddens me, is that the animals are in a separate realm to humans in Spirit. I have not experienced this. I sense that there is no separation of any kind in Spirit. If everything is instantaneous, a thought away and wrapped in love, I can't understand how anyone can say that the animals are not with us in Spirit. Never in my communications have I experienced having to search elsewhere for an animal or person as if they were separate.

So you are aware, it is never an interruption to connect with your animal in Spirit either. They can multitask so to speak, they can be busy doing their job or whatever they are doing in Spirit and be able to connect as well.

In the meantime, while they are in Spirit, they can be busy doing jobs of all kinds. Or they can be resting up after a hard life or healing. Time is not of the essence here. So, what may feel like a few seconds to them, can be years to us in our linear time.

To give you one example, here is a dog helping heal someone in Spirit

In one communication with a boxer, I connected with him a few months after he had transitioned. As I let the scene come to life in my mind's eye, there he was with a man, standing by a lake, surrounded by trees and a cabin by the lake side.

There, the man was throwing the ball and the boxer bound in the water to retrieve the ball. It happened again and again. He noticed me and said 'Look, tell Mama I am here with Rich, it's so fun, he can just keep throwing and throwing the ball, I keep getting the ball and it happens again! He never gets tired and neither do I!' He was so excited as he was letting me know this.

I asked him why he was with this man Rich. He answered with 'He always wanted a dog in his life and he had a pup once, his first dog of his own. She was in an accident when she was four months old and she passed. He was heartbroken and never got another dog. He always loved me though and I love him too. So I am helping him heal his hurt and stay by his side for now.

When I conveyed what I had been shown and what had been explained, it all made sense to his person. She had said goodbye to her good friend and neighbour Richard or Rich a few years prior when he passed on from a terminal illness and yes he had lost a dog a long time ago, when she was a young pup and never could get another one. These two were always happy to be together in body and he always loved fetching the ball and playing in water, so it warmed her heart to know they were with each other in Spirit now.

The animals can have the job of being a guide to your animals here with you, a guide to the new animal coming to you as well. They could be helping you on your journey from in Spirit also. Some animals have shown me looking after litters of pups in Spirit. Other animals take care of children or other animals. Often when I am sharing what the animals are doing in Spirit, it is in alignment for their personality and who they were here on Earth.

A sweet older labrador girl in Spirit, had been in Spirit for a few months, she had lived a long life and had been enjoying her rest. She let me know she was now helping Mama with the pups. She said that it was a lot of work for her and wanted to help. She showed me her sitting in between two cheeky pups that were getting rough when playing biting games and both were needing a sleep. She just sat right in the middle of them and they were standing with what looked like an empty space between them. This is what it looked like in reality. When I described this to her human, she said that she had always thought her girl would have been a great mother. She laughed when I described what I had been shown because this space between them happened a few times already. Now she knew it was her.

For one horse, her new job in Spirit, at that moment, was to welcome horses into Spirit that had been euthanised. She showed me welcoming the horse and walking with them across a huge field and as they walked, it gave the newly transitioned horse time to adjust to what had just happened for them. By the time they had reached a certain point in walking, the horse now was aware of being pure energy once more and the joy I felt from this horse was immense.

The animals have been clear in showing me that they simply cannot get stuck here on earth in our realm. They do not have any misunderstandings as to what is happening, unlike humans, nor do they have other explanations or worries to grapple with and so they transition smoothly into the next realm. It can happen that if an animal has had an accident or in shock, they can be disorientated. Sometimes a lost animal will remain by their physical body until they are found but they will always have someone guide them back to Spirit. If you do get a sign from your animal, such as hearing them or seeing them, they are letting you know they are ok and yes you did hear what you did and you did see what you thought you saw, in case you are questioning it right now. If someone is feeling as though their animal is around and not leaving, it will be either your fears creating a loop kind of experience that is residual energy or because they are coming back often and keeping a loving eye out on you. It is not because they can't leave. Again, time is irrelevant in the Spirit realm. A few more days with you is like seconds for them in Spirit.

The Spirit realm has no restrictions in time and distance and no density in form. I sense it is gentle but not slow and nothing is hard or about force in any way. If we can imagine what it would be like to be in Spirit in this form without the use of fingers or anything physical how would we let our loved ones know we are around and we are ok? Thoughts can be sent to us. There is no language in Spirit, we communicate through thoughts and it is the same with the animals. The word for this is telepathy. Many people right away, associate the word telepathy, to mind control but it is not that at all. Telepathy is communication from one mind to another by extra sensory means. Believe it or not you most probably have experienced this yourself at one time or another. Have you ever answered a question you thought someone had asked but they actually didn't, they were thinking of it though? Both of you may be a bit surprised. Or you can sense what another person's train of thought about something is? Maybe you have thought of someone and the next day they reach out to you? If you are anywhere else time wise in your thoughts, such as thinking of the past or thinking of the future, you can miss out on when your animal pops in. If we take the time to check in what we are thinking and how we are thinking, your animal has a better opportunity to pop in.

Imagine you are thinking of the weekend plans coming up, you think to yourself, I have to remember soccer training on Saturday morning, 8am, then a lunch bbq with family, oh I need tomatoes, gosh when I am going to be able to do that?... (a thought pops in of your animal in Spirit in the kitchen next to you)... what do I make for dinner tonight? You think back to when you were younger, weekend mornings of team sport activities and how rushed it all was, you think to yourself, am I doing a good job.... (an image of your animal and you relaxing together pops in)... oh I remember how that felt, I miss them so much, having those cuddles. Sigh... now what was that thing I had to do and forgot to write down... Twice, the animal tries to send their person some love, showing they were right there in the kitchen at that moment and even sent a memory in the mix to remind her of when they would relax together. Unfortunately, you have now rushed off to do the next thing and these two attempts were missed.

I will give you another example and you may even recognise this as something you may have experienced yourself. I am going to ask you to picture a dog in your mind, it can be any kind of dog because this your imagination after all. Let's give this dog a name, we can call him Ralph. Now imagine a woman. She has been missing her dog Ralph that transitioned a few months ago. He really wants his person to know he is right here because she has been so stressed and hurting. This person is into the next day and Ralph tries again, as he really wants to let her know he is around. While busily running errands, people are having a conversation, as she passes them, someone mentions the name Ralph. She thinks to herself, I miss my Ralph… She walks into a shop and at the entrance are little keychains with children's names, her eyes lay right on one with the name Ralph. Ok, she thinks to herself, that's a bit weird? The next night, she goes to watch a movie with her partner, only to learn the main characters name is Ralph. She turns to her husband and says, "I've seen Ralph's name and heard it over the past few days, do you think it's a sign?' Her husband replies 'It's probably a coincidence because you are missing him.'

There is Ralph in Spirit saying "Dad! No! Come on!! I am really trying here!" A few days later, her 10-year-old son comes home from school, with a book he has borrowed from the library, he explains the book to his Mom and says 'The book is about a boy named Charlie and he meets a new best friend, guess what his name is Mum? He smiles so big as he says the name 'It's Ralph.' This one hits her heart; she knows it isn't wishful thinking and it isn't imagination! Ralph is definitely letting me know he is around. Thank you bud for letting me know you are here! Love you so, so much! Ralph in Spirit is super happy with himself, his mum finally got the love message from him.

To give another example

A golden retriever in Spirit knows his Mama misses him still.
It was the first vacation that the couple were going to have

since their dogs had transitioned. She was thinking to herself how strange it all was, to not have to organise a pet sitter, or go through the routine with anyone, buying treats for while they were away, looking at sad eyes as she packed her suitcase. None of that this time. Instead it was a simple pack your suitcase and off we go. She was driving with her husband on the freeway, thinking of how much she missed her love, she tried hard to not let a tear out. Looking out the window of the passenger side, a semi drives up next to them. It is big and yellow. It has her attention, she watches the truck as it slides up beside them and going a fraction faster, she notices writing on the side and reads it. There on the side of the truck in the biggest letters ever is her boy's name! She has a heart moment, notices the colour yellow which to her personally, means happiness and hope. She can't explain how she knew it but she knows by how it feels for her, that he wanted to let her know he was around her. Had it have been 10 minutes later; she would not have seen the truck or her boy's name. If she was asleep, she would have missed it too, but he made sure she got the sign!

The animals already don't have fingers or dexterity in their physical bodies which must be most annoying for them at times. So now in Spirit, they don't have any physicality whatsoever about them. How can they let you know they are around you when they visit? We have just discussed the way they can be around us through thought. They can also send signs and all sorts of magical things can happen, so let us explore some. The way they can send signs and how they can do this is countless to be honest. As you read, be curious and you can see if you have already had a sign already.

LOVE SIGNS FROM YOUR ANIMAL

The signs are not random. They are love, learning to show you without a body.

As I said before, the animals can send us so many signs in so many various ways that I am unable to list all the ways.

I will share with you some examples of what I have experienced with clients as an animal communicator and in my own life and these are only a few. Hopefully you will have your own version of your heart knowing a sign from your animal.

You see, you have had your own individual relationship and experience with your animal, and this can include what kind of sign your animal will send you too. We can question whether it is just a wish or an actual sign from our animal. I ask for confirmation from my animal or those in Spirit and you can ask your animal in Spirit too. I find it is usually a huge confirmation for me if I see or get the same thing, three times. Again, you ask for what you need, to know it is true for you.

Many people are aware now of signs from loved ones in Spirit coming to us here on Earth as feathers, songs, dragonflies, butterflies, coins, numbers, the list goes on.... Very often, the animals in Spirit will use other animals to let you know they are sending you a love sign. You may notice an animal giving you an extra-long look or an insect hanging around a few seconds or minutes longer than usual. This is from your animal.

Dragonflies

I once had one client be disappointed that her cat in Spirit was letting me know he would send a dragonfly to her, for her to know it was from him. The client thought it was a common sign and wondered why he would choose a dragonfly of all things. Her cat said he had chosen a dragonfly because she already knew that this was a clear sign of a loved one from Spirit and wanted her to get something obvious in her awareness. A few days later I had a message from her, she expressed her disappointment that it was not more original in the communication but was prepared to look out for a dragonfly. She continued to explain that in her area where she lives, she takes her dogs to a particular beach. For two years she has been coming to this beach. One morning at the beach, she steps out of her car, ready for a walk with the dogs and flying around her head is the biggest dragonfly she has ever seen, not only the biggest dragonfly but the very first dragonfly she has ever seen at this beach! It stayed for a good 10 minutes until it registered that it was a sign from her cat, as he had said in the communication. He continues to send her dragonflies at random times.

A clever doberman boy in Spirit, wanted to let his Mum and her partner know that he was around them and happy they had found each other. He let me know, to tell Mum that a black and red dragonfly would show up and that her partner would be the one to notice the dragonfly. A few months later I had a message from her with a photo of a black and red dragonfly. Her partner was washing the car and there on the bonnet of the car was the dragonfly, it sat there and watched as he was polishing the front of his car. He noticed it right away.

Feathers

In a communication with a precious female dog, she showed me the home that she lived in when she was in body. Her Mum and her would go on nature walks together on their property and it was a favourite thing for them both to do. As I described what I was seeing, her Mum was very surprised as I had described the exact steps and location of her walk that morning. I was then shown a white feather and that it was her sign. I asked her Mum about the white feather and she reached over and showed me one right there at that moment "You mean this one that I picked up this morning while on my walk?' Every time her Mum finds a random white feather, she thanks her love out loud for the love sign.

Brown Feathers from Violet - Little Violet had been in Spirit a few months when she let me know to tell her Mum that she would be sending two brown feathers as a sign. Each time her Mum found one, she is to see it as a very big I love you from Violet. Two days after I gave the message from Violet, her Mum found the first brown feather!

Yellow Butterflies

In a communication with a golden retriever in Spirit, her sign for her Mom was going to be yellow butterflies. I described the scene that was shown to me. A water fountain at a park and the arrival of one little yellow butterfly which then becomes a whole flood of yellow butterflies. I have to give the client what I am shown and so felt sad when I was told that there is no such park in her area or that she goes to and she has never seen a water fountain that fit my description, yellow butterflies are not common in her area either. I thought to myself that I have to trust what the animal gives me all the same. I received a message a few months later from this client. Her first words were 'You are not going to believe this...' I love these words and I read some more. She wrote, our family went to visit family a few hours away, we went by car. On the way back about two hours away from our home, we stopped so the children could stretch their legs. We were at a park so they could run and have a play. I noticed a water fountain but didn't think anything of it. I then noticed one yellow butterfly land on this water fountain, then another and another, until it was covered in butterflies. It then hit me what you had said was going to be a sign from my beautiful girl. It was so amazing and I had tears to know that she had sent this sign of love just for me.

Red Ribbon

A precious staffordshire female in Spirit and her special sign she let me know she was sending her Mum was a random red ribbon. I shared the communication and could feel this girl's excitement now that her Mum knew what the sign was. On a walk with her dog brother, her Mum noticed something on the ground where her brother had stopped. There was a random red ribbon. He had stopped by the side of a creek and just as they sawthe red ribbon on the ground, swimming up to the bank were baby turtles! If she hadn't had stopped for the ribbon she would have missed the baby turtles too. Then a few weeks later, this beings Mum was beginning a new position for work and was doubting herself. As she got out of the car she noticed another red ribbon on the driveway. She picked it up and thought of her girl, when she went inside, the portrait of her girl,which normally rests upright on display had fallen face down. Smiling, she picked up the portrait looking at it as she put it back where it belonged. She knew it was a message just for her that she has got this with her new job and she is being loved and looked out for.

Avengers

I had a client get in touch when his boy a strong staffy male was in Spirit and in the communication, he let his Dad know he would send the sign of the Avengers. His Dad didn't even like the Avengers. He showed me how much he loved his Dad and wanted him to believe in himself and see himself how his boy did. It was the next year, so some time after this communication that the client contacts me. He is explaining to me that he just went for an interview for a new job and didn't know if he could get it and he really wanted it. He describes to me the interview. During the conversation not really related to anything, the person interviewing my client, mentions the Avengers! He called me because he was so shocked and asks, was this my boy? It sure was! He was making sure his Dad was reassured that he was loving him from where he is and that he is being looked out for. It was mind blowing and comforting for my client to have this special sign at this time.

Sunflowers

Our cat Molly let me know she would send our family a sign with sunflowers. I let the family know that this was her sign for us all and to keep an eye out. Nothing for a few weeks even though all of us were waiting with anticipation. One morning, my daughter has a friend come over with a bunch of flowers as a thank you for her. The flowers were sunflowers. A drawing that had gotten lost under the bed made its way out of the abyss under there. It is the same day, the drawing is a sunflower. Later on that evening, I am listening to a playlist made for me by Spotify. I play it in our kitchen as we are preparing our dinner. As we are listening, on comes the song 'You're a sunflower'. We all had tears, as we knew that it was a sign from our precious Molly.

I am with her at work every day.

In a communication with a beautiful dame of a cat, at 19 years she was a true lady. She showed me her life with her Mum, a long and happy life and so much love between them. She informed us that she would be going to Spirit soon but would be looking out for her Mum still. She showed me her Mum achieving something really big and being successful. She said to me very clearly 'I am with her at work every day'. I am shown cream walls and I ask her Mum if she brought her cat to work with her, at the time of the communication. The answer is no. Two years later I discover that the cat's human mum, has opened up a tattoo studio! She is booked out solid. I make an appointment and go and see her. As I walk in, I see a portrait photo of her cat. The tattoo studio is named after her cat too. Now I understand what I was shown and told by this precious being. There she is, at work with her Mum every day! I walk into the salon and as I sit in the chair, I only then notice the cream walls that I saw in the communication.

My Red Ball.

I communicated with a beautiful staffy female, she has been in Spirit for 2 weeks now. In the communication she keeps talking about her red ball. When I first mention it, her Mum reaches over and says 'This is the red ball' and shows me. I am happy for this girl, that she knows her red ball is safe. She then lets me know that she will send another sign of her red ball. I interpret this as finding her ball in all kinds of places. Her Mum has a niece who loves this dog so much and misses her, within the next few weeks, she draws a picture for her Aunty. In the picture, there is her niece with her dog and a blue ball, also in the drawing is this beautiful girl with her Mum. Next to her is the red ball.

The animals send you letters to remind you of their name.

Another way the animals let you know they are around is to use the first letter of their name as a sign.

This precious being is a missed and greatly loved Chocolate Labrador. He loves the children in the family and his Mom and Dad so much. In the communication he let me know that he would send his Mom the letter J to let her know it is his name and that he is ok and loves everyone. We finished the communication happy to know the intention for his family. One evening the young boy of the family is getting ready to do some colouring in. He isn't sure what to colour so he lets the alphabet colouring book open and choose for him. It falls on the letter J. His Mom knew right away what this meant .

Bea is in Spirit wanting to let her Mom know she is around her especially the last month. My client mentions she has been seeing the letter B in the weirdest places. In a really obvious way the B will make its way into her awareness. Bea said that yes this was her and to prove it she would send a big glitzy B her way. Bea did indeed send her Mom a glitzy B. A few weeks later, as she walked into a department store, there on the stand was a big B covered in diamontes.

Sounds from the Animals

When the animals send sounds I am always fascinated! To think that they are in that realm, no more physicality about them and yet we can hear sounds.

A very cheeky boy dog who has been in Spirit for a few weeks, knows his people are missing him. He tells me he has been flipping his silver food bowl at night. I see what he means when he shows me the bowl flipping. He shows me where the big bag of dog food is too and how he managed to tip it over. He was feeling pretty clever. When I mentioned this to my client, there was laughter and tears. Yes, they had heard the bowl flipping in the kitchen in the middle of the night. They knew it was him because flipping his bowl, was how he would let them know it was time for him to eat, when he was in body. This cheeky boy was also well known for tipping the bag of dog food too.

Many people have heard their animal walking in the house, hearing them exactly in the way that they used to when they were in body. Often in communications, there has been an extra set of claws clicking on the tiles or the floorboards confirming for the person, it was their animal. Often there are scratches at the door still and meows or whines that can be heard. At nighttime when our conscious mind is not so in charge and especially as we drift off into sleep, this is when these things can happen freely.

For us in our family, my daughter and I were in the kitchen and we heard a loud Molly meow. It was her! We heard it, not once but twice. In that second we both raced to the doorway where we thought we heard it, only remembering then, that Molly would not be seen as she was in Spirit. We thanked Molly out loud for the hello.

Another amazing event that happens, is when the animals in Spirit show up and are there with your animal in their final days. Often in these communications, I will describe who I am sensing around the animal who is preparing to go. I will pick up the other living animals in the family as well as the animals in Spirit. It is with great relief and happiness to clients to know that their animal is being waited for and won't be alone in Spirit.

For one family in a communication, I sensed two more dogs that were actually in Spirit. I asked if their house felt really full in the week leading up to having to say goodbye to their dog. Both of them said that yes they did feel it was very busy, they could hear all of the activity downstairs while the people of the home slept. It could not have been the living dogs, as one was quite smaller than these dogs and the other one was having trouble moving about.

I have a bowl of water that is outside in our outdoor area. It is for our dogs to have access to water while they are lounging outside. It sits outside our bedroom door that opens to our outdoor area. It is around 3am and I am woken up by the sloppiest, thirstiest slurps ever and it goes on for what feels like

It can be snoring you might hear, it could be snuffles, it can be a soft whine, whinnying, meow or purr. Next time you suspect you heard something, acknowledge it. Instead of discounting it, what if you, for just a moment, check in with yourself to see if this felt true for you, in what you heard?

For one client, he really missed his cat in Spirit and had been hearing something being knocked off the hall table. A little thud would be heard. Every morning when he would wake up, a cat figurine would be on the floor and he would have to pick it up and put it back in its chosen spot. It was a porcelain figurine and it was important to him, as it was in memory of his cat. When I connected with him, he showed me how clever he was in knocking things over with his paws when he was in body. Paper...swipe, toys...swipe, pens...swipe. Anything on a surface was fair game here. It was no different in Spirit. The soft thud that his Dad heard as the figurine landed on the carpet rug, made this cat happy. He knew he could move this figurine because he had been practicing so much lately and secondly, he wanted his Dad to know, he knew the figurine was for him and that he loves his Dad. His Dad was so happy to know that the sound he heard was his beloved practicing his skills in Spirit and that he knew about the figurine.

Numbers

Many of us now pay attention when we get numbers repetitively. Numbers are a very obvious way that Spirit and those in it are communicating with us. We have numbers daily in our lives already with the date and time for almost everything we do in life. The Animals sending us numbers is a clear way that the animals can send signs to us. It may be that you notice the number/s on number plates, posts on social media, every time you check the time, a book, a sign on the side of the road or when you are on the computer scrolling. Each number has a vibration and meaning to them. If you are open to this then you invite magic from the numbers. Sure, it is a big gift already for the animals to send you numbers, thank them, just know that investigating the meaning behind it can be a special message behind it also, just for your heart to know. It is up to you to trust your intuition as you learn the meaning and the relevance in your life.

For one precious little shitzu in Spirit, in the communication she said to me the number 15. I mentioned it to her people. They were surprised as they told me they had been seeing the number 15 so many times since she had transitioned. Wondering what she was meaning by this number she said it was the date that they would get her gift to them. I said for them to pay attention when the numbers came up in the future. Sure enough when they were ready to get another pup, they brought the little one home and realised it was on the 15th of August.

Hold the Phone

Very often the animals will let you know they are close by and sending you love messages through your phone. If you see repetitive images or numbers pay attention. You could hear their name a few times while watching something. If there are songs that come up repetitively on your phone, listen for three times and follow the curiousity. Look up the lyrics. The animals can send a flurry of their photos to you by memories coming up, or certain quotes come up and make you think of your animal.

Birds

I have had communications where the animals are choosing other animals besides the insects, for their people.

In one communication, I was shown two magpies and when they showed up, the animal wanted their people to know it was a love message from them.

In another communication a bright red cardinal was the sign for one dogs Dad. The cardinal showed up a few weeks later in the backyard.

> *For a client in Romania, she was wanting a confirmation from her animal in Spirit that getting another dog was accepted by her and maybe she could help her find another dog that would be a good fit for her. When I asked what her sign would be, she showed me a red cardinal. My client waited patiently for the sign. A few weeks later, my client had been looking on the internet at rescue dogs, during her search, she went from one website to another and as she clicked on one particular website there was an image of a red cardinal. She then clicked on another site and part of their logo was a cardinal. Her mum was being lead right to where the new animal could be found.*

> *A Pomeranian, in Spirit wanted his Mom to know that when she saw a red cardinal in the backyard that this was a sign from him. In the next few months his Mom knew it was his sign when a cardinal would arrive in the backyard. It has been the same sign over the years and he gets a big thank you every time.*

It can be any kind of animal. It will show up several times for you. When it does, look up the meaning of the animal. There are variations on the internet for the spiritual meaning of animals and so when you are looking, feel for what feels true for you. There are also multiple beautiful animal oracle decks that you can look up the meaning of an animal also. The animals in Spirit can also use the embodiment of another animal also. It is not for always, just for a moment. You will recognise if this could be a visit from your animal by how the animal interacts with you. An extra long look, a look of recognition or maybe lots of licks. Your heart will notice it first and it could be only for a fleeting moment.

As you have seen in these examples, the animals can send all kinds of signs to you. The way you will know it was your animal, is how are you feeling in that moment and to be aware of what you think of first, when you come across it. If it is your animal that you think of, it is from them. The sign could have triggered a memory or maybe even a smile.

Visiting hours

Another way the animals can let us know they are around , is when they visit us while we sleep. They can come to lay with us on the bed. Remember how it felt when your cat would walk on your bed or your dog would rearrange themselves to get comfortable for sleeping? You may feel these kinds of movement or have impressions left on your bed from your animal visiting. You may even find that in your state of sleep you are in a state of forgetfulness and notice your animal but your mind hasn't had the chance to explain it away yet.

> *As I slept one night, I remember turning over and telling Gordon my dachshund to please move over. In my sleep, I moved him and even thought to myself, how heavy he is every time I move him. I go back to sleep after I have moved him. The next morning, I think back to what happened during the night, to realise that yes I had moved Gordon physically and literally. Yes Gordon was in Spirit also.*

Previously we discussed being able to pick up a scent from Spirit. Our loved ones that are people can send us scent to help us think of them. A certain scent of perfume? Or a smell of cigar if they liked to smoke cigars. The animals can do this also. Keep your nose out for scents.

One little dog in Spirit wanted to be sure to send the smell of sausages on a barbecue. He loved the smell of this when it was family barbecues and would always wait for his piece of sausage every time.

In Spirit he sent his family this scent, there was a waft of cooked sausages and then it was gone. No one around the family's home was barbecuing at this time either. Was it their dog? When I connected with this little guy, in the communication I could smell this sausage too! When I asked if they had been picking this smell up also, they were so happy to have their suspicions confirmed that it was indeed their little dog.

Coffee cups

Take a moment to look in your tea or coffee cup for a sign. I love my morning cup of coffee, the aroma of the coffee is a welcoming scent for me to sit and enjoy my cup. I love this time too because for me, this is also how the animals connect with me. It can be a heads up for who is coming into my awareness for a communication. It can also be a message from a particular animal for me, seeing different animals can bring messages that are encouraging or what I need to know for the day. If you drink coffee, have you looked in your coffee cup at all?

Songs

Often in communications the animals will bring to my awareness songs and music. If you have ever had a song on replay in your head? Did that song make you think of your animal at all? That is a message from your animal to you.

A client who had only recently said goodbye to her precious boy, was hurting and missing her boy so much! All this client wanted was to see him again. We were messaging back and forth about this topic and talking about her love's involvement with this. As I was typing the song on the speaker came on, at that moment with the words 'Dream a little dream of me.' My client set out the intention to dream of her boy.

In a communication with a little terrier, he showed me dancing with his Mama and how much he loved her and knew how much she missed him. I could hear 'What a wonderful world' it kept repeating in my head. I thought of Louis Armstrong right away. When I asked the client if this song meant anything to her it was a no. I left it at that and finished the communication. A few minutes later I get a message from the client. She was in disbelief that she didn't think of this before in the communication. The dancing I was shown, was her dancing with him in her arms, practicing for her upcoming wedding. The words 'What a wonderful world' were the words in the mashup song that they would dance together to, as it was the chosen wedding song for my client!

Now you are aware of some of the ways that the animals can send us love messages. It is really unlimited in the many ways that they can do this. The best way for you to know that it is a sign from your animal, is to listen to your heart and be aware if you are noticing something and if your animal comes into your thoughts, you can be sure they are trying to connect with you. The most helpful and easiest way for your animal, is for you to be open to any signs that your animal wishes to send you. They can be subtle in how they happen and so your animal may help you out and send the same sign again and again until you get that it was from them. You may find that writing down when you get the signs in a journal, can be reassuring and even fun for you. It can be something you look back on in case your life gets busy, and you forget. This is a beautiful reminder to look at to remind you that it did happen and can happen again.

You also can ask them to send you a sign that you would know, you certainly don't need someone else to tell you what a sign can be. However this has to be requested with ease, you don't need to know the how, or when it will happen, just the what.

If you would like to try this for yourself, firstly check what your truth is about this first. Do you believe that the animals can really send you a sign? Be honest because if you feel it can only happen for others and not for you, then so it is. Your intention matters here. If you are doing this to only test, then you could be waiting for a while.

If you truly want a sign, then from your heart, you can ask them to do this. Please don't put a time limit on it either, now you know the effort that goes in to being able to do this. People can get so frustrated when they have been waiting for a sign and it seems to never come. Some people even think that their animal has forgotten them. No, your animal has not forgotten you, they cannot forget you. When this happens and you are frustrated, creativity, imagination and curiosity cannot flow in this state. This is the moment where you can let go of the need for anything to happen. Go and do something else. Think of something entirely different. You may be pleasantly surprised when something magical happens, when you were least expecting it.

Just like when you put an order in when you are dining in a restaurant, you choose something off the menu and give your order and then you wait. You have a drink, some conversation and in the meantime, your meal is being prepared. You don't expect it to be there in five minutes or follow the wait staff into the kitchen, to then instruct the chef on how to make your meal. You leave it up to them. It is the same with the animals sending a sign. Leave it to them.

Have fun with this! Making this fun, keeps it light and this can make it so much easier for your animal to send the sign and for you to be able to receive it. Ask for your sign and then wait with expectation and anticipation that your animal is going to do this for you. I for one, will always celebrate how clever your animal is and how happy I am for you!

Staying Connected

We can think that the animals have no clear way of responding to our requests of communication and if we feel like our intuition is weak or not working properly then what hope is there?

I am happy to let you know that you have tools and ways that can work for you. Try one and see. We are going to need to have your imagination please. Be open to receiving the information through your imagination. As we do this, remember to keep things light energetically.

Keep it simple.

Meditation

When you sit down to meditate, as you are relaxing and getting into the state of peacefulness. Ask your animal to come and join you. Have your awareness around you and see if you can sense when the energy shifts. It may feel different on one side of you, it could be in front of you. Where is the shift and what does it feel like? Can you see your animal in your minds eye? Can you hear them? You can ask your animal to move away and then move closer to practice recognising their energy. Always thank them when they do show up.

Listening and writing.

You may like to try listening for your animal. You now know that an animal has their own intelligence and their own thoughts. You know too that they can communicate telepathically. Here is something that you can try.

Sit down with a candle to set the intention that this a sacred moment. Open to a page in your journal or on a piece of paper. Ask your animal a question, again, please keep it simple and light to begin. A question might be 'What do you want me to know today?' then stop and listen for an answer. Catch it quickly. Write it down before anything. It may be one word. It may be a sentence. Or it could be a whole lot of information coming in, write it all down first. Is it a scene coming up in your mind? Is it a memory? Write it down. Is it an object? A colour? A number? Catch it. Then you can look at it and analyse if you need or you can allow your heart to know it's a message for you, from your animal.

Oracle Cards

A tangible and fun way is to use oracle cards. There are so many different oracle cards available. Choose one that really appeals to you. If you have a strong sense in clear seeing, then visual cards with beautiful artwork will appeal more to you. For those of you who feel, take the time to choose a deck that feels good for you. Those of you who just know, well you know what to do to choose yours.

Set the intention to work with your animal with this deck. Light your candle and be calm in your heart.

Ask your animal 'What do I need to know from you today?' Then shuffle and pull a card.

No put backs. Look at the card in front of you, there may be a word or a message, what relevance does this have for you in this moment? Look at the card and see what you are drawn to in the card. Is it a colour? Perhaps the next time you look, you are drawn to an object, or a flower. Pay attention to where your eye is drawn and what it means for you. Can you hear anything when you look at the card? Can you feel something?

Have fun with this.

You may want to write the meaning down and be curious of what this can mean for you for the day or over a week.

DREAM A LITTLE DREAM OF ME

And above all, watch with glittering eyes the whole world around you because the greatest secrets are always hidden in the most unlikely places. Those who don't believe in magic will never find it."
— Roald Dahl

To dream of your animal and have a visit together is one of the most longed for experiences for you with your animal I know. Thankfully it is possible, so if you haven't dreamt of them yet, please know it can and will happen. Sleep is so very important as you are healing for all the physical benefits but also for the opportunity to experience connection this way. Many of us just want to know our animal is ok for ourselves, to see and feel it for ourselves. Be honest as to what your intention is behind wanting to see your animal. Of course, it is because you love them but is it because you feel you can't live without them? Do you need reassurance and are still unable to move on emotionally? Or are you curious as to how they are? Will your heart be on its own healing journey and this can ease the unknown by seeing your animal again? If you have been trying to have a dream and have been asking, please know the animals can hear you and they know and believe me they are trying. What can you do to help them? When we are asleep, we are in between worlds of our reality and other realms. In this space, anything can happen. Your part of the brain that can cancel out whether what happened was real or not is quiet. In this space, your animal can send messages to you and visit you.

In dreams is the perfect place for all loved ones including our animals can send messages of love to us. Are you sleeping deeply? To ensure you have a good sleep is a great place to start. I have already shared what can be done to help previously, so please take another look in chapter 3 if you need.

Now ask yourself what do you believe about the animal's ability to come to you in a dream? See if you can catch a limiting belief around this. If you do catch one, such as it can never happen to me. Let's change that. Can you change this to maybe this could happen for me? Leave it open as a possibility. When you are ready you can set the intention that you will see your animal in a dream and kindly ask them before you sleep. Now, I understand often we expect it to happen that very night, simply because we asked. It doesn't happen like that though sometimes it can. The animals also have free will and time is not relevant where they are. So be open to be ready. The other thing to be mindful of is how much thought energy is going towards this wanting? If there is too much energy of worrying, anxiety, stress, disbelief, anger or sadness, this can contribute to delaying the dream happening. So please gently set your intention and be peaceful as you can knowing it will happen at the right time. These things can't be forced or rushed in any way. Spirit is powerful but gentle and in flow. So whenever is the right time, is the perfect time for you to have a dream.

Something that you can try is to say a thank you for your animal before you sleep. It is a simple act and can open the gateway for them to visit. The animals are on a very high frequency no longer being in physical form. We are on a lower frequency in our physicality and then with our thoughts and emotions. It's like we need to step up to their level and they need to step down a little to reach us. The way we can get closer to their frequency that they are vibrating on, is to be in a state of gratitude. So before you close your eyes, place your hand over your heart and think of your animal. Close your eyes if you need. Let their beautiful face come into your mind's eye. Think of all the love you have for your animal and let that grow your heart even bigger. On that note with this feeling, you can ask 'Please come see me tonight while I sleep. I love you so much and would love to see you when you are ready' You can also have a quiet word to yourself as well, saying I intend to remember my dreams clearly. Maybe you have to do this a few times so go gently each time and heartfelt every time you connect with your heart. Then stay in a state of curiousity and allowing. In their time, not yours. It will happen.

For one client, after a communication with tears running down her face, she asked me how she could dream of her animal, she had such a longing to know he was ok. I shared this information with her. Two days later I received an email with a heartfelt thank you. She said she finally had a dream of her boy; she actually felt him and hugged him and had tears when she woke up. My client was so grateful to have had the experience, and her heart was at peace knowing he was totally fine! Clients have sometimes been distressed when they have dreamt of their animal but the dream was terrifying. There could have been a sense of helplessness or despair with your animal in your dream. Sure, you saw them but there was nothing that could be done to save them. Sometimes the dreams we have, are sorting out feelings and emotions from our subconscious mind, if what you experienced with your animal was distressing or very stressful then you may still be sorting yourself out in your dreams. This is not a visitation from your animal. The message and feeling from your animal will always be with the intention to be a message of love. You will have to trust your intuition in interpreting the dream. Perhaps it is giving you clues on what still needs your care and attention as you are healing. It can be helpful to keep a dream journal. There is no need to make this complicated. Just a notebook and a pen by your bedside. When you wake up, jot down the dream.

It can be as simple as doing in bullet form.

- Date

- Who was in the dream?

- Where was the dream?

- What did I see in the dream?

- Who was I in the dream?

- Who else was in the dream?

- How do I feel about it?

- What do I think it might mean?

When you do this practice then when it happens with your animal you will have caught the experience as well. If you don't want to do this then please at least record it somehow for yourself when you do dream of them.

For me personally I had a very vivid dream of a dog in my life named Simba. He was our neighbour's dog but often stayed with us at our house and I adored this dog. He was the fluffiest, big eared and big pawed German Shepherd puppy, who grew into the most regal,l handsome adult dog. I would tell him every time how handsome he was and give him big belly rubs and love. At the time of the dream, I was living in Canada.

The last time I saw Simba was a few months before, when I visited my previous home where he lived. We had this ritual we did. When we would get off the bus from school, we would run from his place up to our place and he looked forward to this every day. Simba developed bad hip pain. The last visit was no different, he wanted to run, so we went slowly as we ran together one last time, before I went to Canada.

One night I had a dream of Simba, he showed himself as the vibrant young dog he used to be. I was surprised but so happy. I saw he was jumping and play bowing. No sore hips! I hugged him with tears of pure love and happiness. We are back at his place and he is ready to run. We run together, except this time, he continues running past my house in the dream and I cried. My heart knew he wasn't going to run with me again in reality. He was no longer there. I woke up with tears and a heavy heart.

I called my mum to see if she could check in on him, to confirm my dream. She ran into a family member just a few days later and asked how he was. They told her that Simba had sadly passed away just a few days before. When she let Mum know what day and time. I worked out that just after he transitioned, I had the dream. So even though I was all the way in Canada he still let me know.

When the animals show you themselves, often you will see them as their younger self. They are no longer in physical form but they show you this, so you know they are in their new life and in perfect health and in no more pain. When they visit you in a dream it will feel very real and you will know you had a visit with them. They will always come to let you know they love you and miss you too. They want to reassure you they are ok. They may communicate with you telepathically, exchanging words in thoughts to you with a special message. Be in a state of acceptance and know it's for you. Sometimes other family members or loved ones may dream of your animal before you do. Please know there may be a special message for you via the person, maybe just hearing that they showed up in a dream looking how they did is comfort for you. Your turn will come too.

Setting our intentions clearly for our wanted dream is always helpful. One way to do this can be by saying an affirmation. An affirmation that you might like to try or as inspiration to create your own could be

I now have a deep and peaceful sleep, knowing my animal can come to me in a dream tonight. My heart is full of love and gratitude for the moments we share together. I am so excited knowing this will happen at the perfect time for me.

WHAT JUST HAPPENED?

Until one has loved an animal, a part of one's soul remains unawakened
— Anatole France

The above quote is true and hopefully by now because of what you have read and for how much you loved your animal, you are aware and thinking and paying attention to your healing and your heart and soul is becoming a much more important part of your everyday life.

Many people are curious as to how to explain some of the strange events that happen after their beloved animal has transitioned. A person may want to share with me how in one particular look into their new animal's eyes, they are sure they saw their animal in Spirit. Or they express their surprise at how much their new animal has similarities to their animal in Spirit.

They will be shocked at the synchronicities that led them to their new animal or even how their new animal made their way to them.

I must clarify here that yes reincarnation does happen and I will devote a whole chapter to that and share with you some amazing experiences. However not every animal comes back. This is does not mean they don't love you in any way or that you have done anything wrong.

The animals with their soul wisdom and insight may just want to rest for a while in Spirit. It is not easy at all coming to this Earth for both humans and animals. A rest is well deserved after a big life here. It may also be time for another animal to come into your life. Your animal may have left at the time they did, in order for this other animal to make its way to you and fulfil their purpose and you with theirs too. As I am writing this, it brings me to the point of people feeling guilty about thinking of another animal or the possibility of getting another animal. People think they are in some way betraying their animal in Spirit. The animals in Spirit are overjoyed at you being able to love another animal. They would never be upset with you or feel as though you betrayed them. Even if your animal in Spirit disliked being with other animals in body, being in Spirit brings changes in attitudes and understandings. The animals have shown me how heavy their people's hearts are or can be, when they have so much love inside to give and no one to give it to. Please know that your animal is having a say in who is coming to be with you and perhaps even guiding you in bringing you and the animal together and supports the perfection of it all.

The animals know that the next animal on the way to you, whenever that is, is going to fulfil their purpose with you in body as well. It is this animal's unique journey and experience and an entirely different relationship and love than what you experienced with your previous animal. Even if it is the soul of your previous animal, the individual personality and lessons are uniquely this animal's.

In a communication with a pit bull in Spirit, he showed me how he was happy with the two dogs that had come to be with his Mom after he transitioned. He would visit often and guide these two. I saw him walking right alongside the male pup and was visually shown him as light filled, almost a watercolour kind of effect to signify he was in Spirit but very much still there in that moment.

I have a client whom I have communicated with for over 4 years. This being was in Spirit for a few weeks when we connected with him. He was excited to let his Mom know that there was a foster dog coming her way. A friend would let her know about him and please could she say yes to taking this dog. He would remind her of him and would be someone she could give her love to and help her heal. His mom was dropping something off at a friend's place. She works at a rescue. Her friend said she didn't want to overstep but had someone to show her. She said this little guy reminds me so much of your little guy! He needed a foster home as he was rescued from a kill shelter. When she saw him she knew that this was the dog that her dog in Spirit had an agreement with and that he was meant to be with her. This little guy had so many similarities to her love in his behaviour and temperament! I am happy to say that this new little one has his forever home with my client and my little mate in Spirit is so very happy for them both.

Soul over

You may have looked at your animal and as you are looking at them you just feel like you are looking into the eyes of your animal in Spirit. They feel just like your loved animal in Spirit in that moment. You have just experienced a soul over. It is the soul of your animal popping into the body of the living animal. No this isn't body invasion, it is an agreement that both animal's souls have with each other. It is momentarily and takes a lot of energy. The purpose for this is to make the physical connection with you for a moment. This is completely by choice of the animal that is living and by the animal in Spirit. This is not a common occurrence as both animals must agree for this to happen. Your intuition will let you know that this has happened for you when it does by if it felt like your animal in Spirit in that moment. Only you can really know this.

> *A beautiful chihuahua female was in Spirit, she had lived a long life with her family and was very much loved and missed. Not a day went by where she wasn't thought of. Time had passed and her Mama had the inspiration to look at getting another chihuahua. Another little girl chihuahua came to join the family. This little one was very different in personality. One night though, her Mama picked the little one up and was looking at her face when all of a sudden, her face looked exactly like her little girl in Spirit. Her nose seemed shorter and her eyes seemed different as well. It only lasted a few minutes. Her Mama questioned if she was going crazy. I explained about the soul over and she felt relieved that no she wasn't going crazy and yes this is a real thing.*

Walk ins

Sometimes the animals in Spirit have an agreement with another animal. It may be that this soul in the new animal has fulfilled their purpose at a young age already, so the animal in Spirit has the opportunity to take over the physical body. No this animal does not transition, the body remains fully intact and living. The soul of the animal in Spirit then takes residence in the body.

It can take a period of time for the behaviours of the first soul to no longer exist and for the soul in Spirit to fully embody the physical aspect of the animal. When the changes begin this is when the person can recognise odd likenesses between the living animal and the animal in Spirit. Depending on how the animals resonate energetically, the adjustment can take a while and this is dependent on getting used to the new vehicle of the body of the animal. It can happen that the animal in Spirit, walks in the body of another animal in a few days or weeks after passing, or in a relative short period of time. It is not a regular occurrence but you will know if this has happened to you by how it feels.

I had a communication with an animal in the Philippines. A dog had just passed after suffering with a terminal cancer. His Mom had contacted me because something baffling had just happened to her. Her dog was laid to rest and was cremated. At the cremation, in walks a puppy off the street that looks just like her dog when he was little. This pup comes inside and sits on the feet of my client and will not move. She pats him while she is there. It is time to go, and the pup insists on coming with her. He stares at her intently and so she picks him up and decides to take him home. When she gets home, this pup knows exactly where to go to pee and does so. He also knows where the door is to go inside and waits for her to open it, just like her dog used to. She is so surprised when he goes to take a drink of water and knows where the water bowl is! He also knows exactly where the bed is and lays down and sleeps. When I asked this soul to show me if he has been here before, he shows me lying on a blue blanket and his Mama singing to him softly as she holds his head, this was his last memory he tells me. I describe what I have been shown by the pup's soul, I then ask the client if this means anything to her. She is crying happy tears, as that is exactly what had happened in the final moments of her dog in Spirits life.

Synchronicities

Have you ever had experiences where there were a few things that happened that seemed random but in flow? Welcome to the magic of synchronicities. Synchronicities are those moments or events where the right person was there at the right time, or you notice the repetition of something. It has meaning to you. The signs or events may not be related in any way but they have your attention.

For one client he kept seeing a blue bow. He had no idea why he even noticed it. He was grieving the loss of his animal and was contemplating getting another pup in the next few months. He noticed a blue bow tied on a gift admiring the radiant blue colour. He saw another blue bow on a child's teddy bear when walking one afternoon. He thought to himself how strange to see a blue bow like this? Thinking it was because he was choosing to notice them, he was very surprised when he went to look at some pups that there were the puppies with bows and there was one with a blue bow. Of course that was the one that came home with him.

I hope after reading this you realise that no, you aren't going crazy if you ever have these experiences and yes this does happen. Listen to your heart first when and if you come across this. Your heart already knows, long before your head has analyzed or tried to understand what has happened.

THE END IS ANOTHER BEGINNING

There is one and the same soul in many bodies
– Plotinus

This is one of my very favourite things to write and talk about and now I get to finally share this with you. As you have read about now, our soul can choose to return to this earth and so it is with the animals. There are some that say this is not possible, you live and you die. Nope not true. Others say that yes it happens but not very often. They say it is very rare. Also not true for me.

If you have had an inkling that you are familiar with your animal and have been since you first laid eyes on them, then this is for you. If you feel that the bond between you and your animal is incredibly real and strong, keep reading. Your soul knows when you recognise another soul you have come across before. It is becoming more common knowledge with past lives with humans thankfully. So it is with the animals too. Again, we are made of energy and our soul is pure energy. Energy does not die nor can it be destroyed ever. It can only be transformed and changed.

When I first started in my journey as an animal communicator, I had no idea what could or couldn't happen. As I have shared before, this topic was certainly not one I was raised to believe in. I wasn't going to allow a ceiling to be put on me about this, about what could or couldn't happen, so in every communication, I was completely open to any possibility. There is a saying I have held close to my heart since I discovered it 'You can hand someone a belief but you can't hand someone a knowing'. I began my journey in animal communication thinking sure it was possible but not until I experienced it myself, did it become my experience and therefore my knowing.

As I have written about Gordon before, I was so very sad when my boy was gone and no longer here with me. We decided to get a boxer dog instead of another dachshund. Mae was such a gift and a loving girl whom we absolutely adore. Sylive our Lhasa Apso was happy to have another dog join our family and the two of them have an understanding and friendship between them. Still, deep inside me was a longing for Gordon, perhaps you have felt this too where you are unsure if you will ever feel a love as big as what you did with your soul animal. It was the same for me.

Having done communications for so many other people all over the world I decided I would ask Gordon myself if he was going to come back to me. It had been 2 years since he had gone to Spirit when I did this. I sat down and connected with Gordy. I know that you could think that my wishful hoping, would make this a yes of course he was coming back. So you know, my husband was against another dog in every way and even I wasn't completely sold on the idea, even though I wanted Gordon back with all my heart. I decided I was going to write down what I recieved from Gordy, I waited to see what happened. I separated myself in a way and pretended I was connecting with another animal in a communication. Clean slate, open heart and I tuned in.

I then sensed Gordy and so I asked my questions, I began well in my composure and then I found myself leaking tears and then decided to let it all go. I ended up pouring my heart out to Gordy on paper. I expressed how much I missed him and not because I wasn't grateful for the animals I have in my life, just that my heart hurt for him. Gordon was full of wisdom for me.

He told me that the personality of Gordon was not coming back to me and that this grief I was feeling for this fact, had to be felt and integrated. I cried, as if all the pain from when it happened came catapulting right back. How can this be? I had done so much work and healing, so I thought. This hurt so much! My Gordy was truly not coming back. Gordon stopped me there. He said that just because that personality with all the quirks and ways of being was no longer, his soul still was and always would be. He let me know we had been together before and would be together again in this lifetime. He explained that he had to wait still a while but that he would be coming back to our family.

Gordon shared that him and I would have a close bond once again but this time he would be the little brother of the family, not the boss dog. He would get on with both Mae and Sylvie. He would be respectful and way less bossy in his behaviour. He would be gentle with Molly our cat also, as he knew she was getting older. Gordon let me know that it would be Dad that would decide on him coming home.

I asked Gordon, how do I find you? He answered that he would ensure I would come across him, I wouldn't actively have to do anything, just follow the nudges. He would be listed as a black and tan male, there would be a choice of two. He would be in a litter of 8 pups. Besides the two boys, all 6 other siblings were girls. His listing would come out of nowhere. It would be the price that Dad was happy to pay. I will know it is him because he will climb on my chest and put his head in my neck how Gordon used to do as a puppy before he got so big.

Ok, so now I have these details, notice there is no particular time frame or location given in this. I now had to trust that I will be nudged in that direction. Even with my indecisiveness in getting another dog, I would be led at the right time. Another 6 months go by and I then decide to start looking at what prices to expect and I question, how do I even feel looking at dachshund puppies? Over the next few months, I would look here and there. No one really grabbed my attention. Life went on in the meantime.

One afternoon a few months later, I decide to have a look on a website and just listed an hour before I look, are two black and tan males. I stop and have a good look at them. One of them gets my attention. I read on about these puppies. In a state of, not really sure what I am doing here, I show my husband. I expect a firm no. Surprisingly, he says to call.

I wasn't expecting that at all. So I call. The woman tells us we can come tomorrow to meet the boys if we like. We sit down as a family and talk about the call and what we are planning to do the next day. I am an animal communicator and so I literally can sense and chat with the pups about their personalities and intentions while in body. I don't know for sure yet if this is Gordon, so I have to wait and see. I am made fun of by the family and some friends when I say this. What do you mean you will wait and see? Who goes to just see a bunch of gorgeous dashchund puppies and not come home with one?

Our family goes the next morning to the address we are given. As we enter the home there, all sleeping quietly, are a litter of 8 puppies. 6 girls and 2 boys. Hang on a minute I tell myself. Just breathe. I remember the connection I had with Gordon but still, it is a possibility that Gordy won't be in this litter. My daughters get down on the floor with the puppies as my husband and I are talking to the people. No puppy is moving from where they are, they are all deep in slumber as the puppies had a vet visit earlier on and were exhausted.

I kneel down to see these beautiful pups closer. One little boy wakes up and runs over to me, he then jumps on me and climbs up to my chest, he puts his head in my neck and lets out the biggest sigh and does not move. The woman is very surprised as someone came to look at this pup just the day before but he didn't show any interest. We have been chosen by this pup. I have never experienced a feeling of 'I am home' from an animal like this before.

My heart is beating fast but still I have to do the right thing by my husband and we have to decide this together. We are told the price to purchase him. It's the price we were wanting.

There isn't really any discussion as we stand together out front and the first words from my husband were 'We are taking him home! He is ours'. That was it! We named him Hugo and he came home with us. I was his mum from that moment on.

I remembered what Gordon had said in the communication, as we brought him inside and introduced him to Sylvie and Mae. Sylvie wagged her tail so happily and she loved him right away. Mae was so happy too! He is the little brother of everyone and he was very respectful and gentle with Molly as well, just as Gordon had told me. I am so happy I had written the communication with Gordon. I found it later that night and showed the family what had been written!

Our family has also experienced moments of soul overs with Hugo. My eldest daughter was looking at Hugo sitting in the door way late one night. He stopped and just looked at her. Usually he runs right up to the bed and insists on being picked up. Not this night. Gordon used to stop in the door way like this. She looks at him and for a few minutes he looks exactly like Gordy. My daughter has tears as she looks at Hugo with so much love and amazed that he looked like Gordon in that moment. Then it is gone. It was as if Gordon wanted to reassure her that inside is Gordy's soul even though he is now Hugo.

Had I not followed the nudges, I could have totally missed this opportunity but I know there would have been another one along the way. This is what I want you to know, if your animal is planning on coming back to you, it will happen! There is no way it won't. However it happens is exactly what was planned and meant to happen. To be given a specific time when asking an animal if they will return, isn't in my experience for the simple reason that you live your life by free will. You may decide on a whim to go travelling and if you are given a specific time for your animal to come then, it could be a major inconvenience. Struggle or pushing is never the intention from Spirit. If your plans change, then their timing and plans can change too. There is ease, perfection and flow from Spirit always. It can be possible though to give you an indication of possibility in a communication when finding out if an animal is coming back.

For one Rottweiler boy, he was planning on coming back to be with his Mum without a doubt. I was asked by her if I could find out when. The answer Kai gave me indicated she would have to wait three years. It would be around October or early November. A big life changing event needed to happen first, before he would come back and she would be meeting a man and falling in love. They would have a great relationship together. He would be the one to suggest getting a puppy. I give the communication and my client is not exactly happy with the time frame or details. The year is 2018 I do this communication. It is then late October 2021, I receive a message. It is the mum of this rottweiler. She writes

When you said it would be three years before I would come across my boy again, I thought it was far too long and that it was all a bit far fetched . I had no interest in any men after bad relationships, so finding another man and falling in love was

not even on my radar. Well, the big life changing event was going through intensive treatment for cancer. I am clear now thankfully. Along the way I did in fact meet a man and we have a great loving relationship. A few weeks ago he started being persistent to look for a Rottweiler puppy. We found one and we are picking him up next weekend. I wanted to let you know.

There it is. 3 years later and the month of October and her love is coming back!

A beautiful Parson Russell terrier in Spirit and had been for a few years now, she was my clients soul dog and there is the biggest bond of love between them. In a communication I was asked to see if she was ever planning on coming back. In the communication I heard the word 'Daisy.' and that this would be a clear sign that this was her. Yellow butterflies would also be a sign that this was her. A few months later I receive a message and my client had lost their other beautiful dog a few months before and were looking for another pup to join the family. They were on their way to go and meet some pups from a new litter of Border Terriers. My client explained to me that when they went to meet the pups, the granddaughter of the breeder was there with the pups. She hands a pup to my client and her husband to hold. As she hands her over she says "I call this one Daisy!'. Both my client and her husband just looked at each other! On their way home they stop at a place and right outside their car door is a yellow butterfly! They did bring the little female home. This being has very similar traits to the precious being in Spirit and I have a communication with her. I ask in the communication that if she is the soul of the one in Spirit, please give me a clear sign so I can let my client know. During the communication I am looking at the current dog's photo and I am given an image of a much-loved black and white teddy bear, I describe this teddy to my client who tells me that no this one does not have a bear like that but her girl in Spirit did! Other bits of evidence were given in the communication and it confirmed for my client what her heart already knew. Her love has come back!

Do you remember the female dachshund from before, when I connected with her in Spirit and she had two very different families and locations?

In a communication a few months later, she let us know that she too was planning on coming back! I asked her how her Mum would know, she said she would be a dapple dachshund, she too would be in a litter of 6 pups and that the woman would reach out to her mum, she wouldn't have to do anything to find her. I saw a love heart too as an image and interpreted that love was around this. She shared she would do similar things as she did in her previous body, so her mum would know it was her. Mom gets a message from a woman letting her know they have a litter of 6 pups. They ask if my client would like to come and see the pups and possibly take one home. My client goes and sees the pups. There is a dapple female pup and they bond right away. The love associated with this was that the word love was in the name of the breeder. She brings the pup home. She fits right in and doesn't let Mum out of her sight just like her love in Spirit, in fact over the next few weeks, this little one does a lot like her soul dog and the bond between them both is evident to the family! They recognise each other's hearts!

If you have suspected that your animal has been with you before I hope this can give you confirmation that it can happen and may have happened for you with your animal. You may be wanting to know what has to happen to have your animal return to you. To begin with, it is accepting that this does not occur for everyone and as much as you are wanting it to happen, it doesn't make it automatic that it will.

Unfortunately, this part is not up to you, you can't make anything happen, not in when it will happen or how it will happen or even if it will happen. It is a hard thing to accept I know. I do know that what you can do, is be open and willing to trust that if it feels right to you to welcome another animal into your heart and life, that this animal is perfect and meant to be with you just as they are. You have nothing to do if your animal is planning on returning to you. Only to follow the nudges when they come. You have more control when you focus on your way of being in this time period.

Your animal may not want to come back in the same species either, so if you are healing and honest with yourself and trusting your inner guidance, it may just happen that even though you are wanting to have your animal return and he was a dog, it could be that the idea of having a kitten has come into your awareness, what if you follow your curiosity in this? Perhaps this kitten is the soul of your dog or is the chosen animal for your journey at this time.

In a communication with a black and white horse who had transitioned, he let me know he was planning on returning. He showed me he loved his person so very much and would rub his head on her to show his affection. He was very clear that he would not be coming back as a horse and instead would be a cat. I smiled at how different the experience would be. He showed me a gorgeous black and white male kitten. He explained he wanted to be in this form so he could go with her.

Do I get another animal?

You have had some time to heal and although the hurt is always going to sting for your animal in Spirit, there may come a time where the thought crosses your mind of getting another animal or you may wonder what your animal in Spirit would think about that. Often people wonder if their animal feels as though they are being replaced. Hopefully now you know, that the uniqueness of each animal and their purpose with you, can never be replaced. This relationship and all the love you share, can never be the same with another animal. This is not to say that you will not love the new animal just as much as your animal in Spirit. Every relationship we have with people that we love has a different kind of love with each person, it is the same with your animals. You can't measure it, you can only feel it.

The animals in Spirit are guiding and loving you from where they are and all they really want is for you to be happy and healing. They know how much love you have to give and they are so happy when they know that an animal can be loved by you, many animals are bursting with love and pride that this animal gets to experience life with you, their people. With the wisdom the animals have, they know that each animal has a purpose and so there is never a need to feel guilt in wanting another animal. It may be that you have decided you can never have another animal again with this heartache. That is totally your choice. Yes, this part with grieving is the hardest of parts and it hurts immensely. Do you also remember every bit of joy and happiness you shared with your animal as well? What of all those moments and love shared between you?

It very well may be, that you honestly don't feel like you could do this again. You will know what is right for you. It can take time to heal and no one else can know the time it will take. What if you could decide that just for now, it certainly isn't an option that feels right, for you to get another animal? For now. Maybe in the future? Who knows? This way you leave the door open to the possibility of maybe welcoming another animal in your life later on.

If you do decide you would like another animal in your life, it is important to be honest with yourself. Are you considering getting this animal because you want distraction from how much your loss hurts? Be gentle with yourself, if this is the case. Have you taken the time and care in your healing journey? You can ask yourself, if you will be able to see your new animal for who they are and accept their differences in ways of being. Will you love them fully without wishing they were your animal in Spirit? If you can answer yes with honesty then by all means go with what feels right!

The animals all have a purpose with you as we have discussed and when and if you do decide to get another animal, you always have your inner guidance to help you on your way.

It is important to also consider if you are fully loving the animals already with you, if you have more than one. Is everyone being loved and seen for who they are? Are they healing in their own grief? The other animals in your family will also appreciate time to heal and adjust to life without their loved one in Spirit. When the time comes and you are considering another animal joining you, it is important to see how the other animal or animals feel about this idea. Where is your other animal in their life stage? Would this be a welcome change for them also? You can utilise animal communication if you want confirmation or are curious as to what your animals are thinking and feeling about the idea. As always trust your intuition and your heart along the way. You will know better than anyone when and if the time is right.

HERE AND NOW

Before they are memory, they are here.

This part of the book is for the animals that are living and with you now and for the ones that are coming to be with you.

The Animals here and now and on their way, they want your heart to know how you can be the best human with them. Let's aim to be a high value human with the Animals. What does this even mean to be high value? A high value human knows that the animals have feelings. They know the animals are unique individuals. They respect the being with them. They are a voice for their animal. They are respectful to their animal in any given situation. They are kind always in intention, in action and in their words. They listen to their animal. They do all they can to help their animal.

They love their animal exactly for who they are and do all they can to understand their animal. They know their animal is here with them for a reason and is present with their animal. They smile at their animal; they encourage their animal. They always see the best in their animal no matter the behaviour. They are quick to say sorry and are prepared to be the best human in their animals' life.

This is what it takes to be a high-level human and trust me when I say that if you could see how your animals see you, despite your shortcomings and imperfections, you would know how valuable you are.

HIGH VALUE HUMAN
TIPS WITH THE ANIMALS

By no means is this all there is to know. Your kindness is key in you coming up with all different ways to show love in action in all circumstances. In all you do and all you say be kind.

1. New Animal.

Having a new Animal come into our life once more can be a mixed bag of emotions. It can make us miss our Animal in Spirit once more. We can be frustrated at times that this new animal doesn't know what our Animal in Spirit knew. What if this was a big mistake you may ask? Please, give it some time and set both of you up for success. Be curious to who this being is. It is all new for them as well. Be clear in your communication and simple and clear in your expectations. Please don't punish them for being an animal and doing animal things. Love them for who they are. Expect the best from them and they will be the best animal they can be.

2. Give them the space and time to settle in.

The Animals have shown me how anxious they feel when they arrive somewhere different or new. I will give a whole chapter for the puppies and the rescue dogs. Please give the animals their space and allow them to come up to you to initiate contact. They will let you know when they would like you to pat them or to be in their space. Let them explore their new space. Let them work out where they feel safe. Make their space warm and welcoming, with the intention that you have set the space up with love. Be clear on where they can go potty. Be clear on where they can sleep. Show them consistently where they eat. Show them where they can relax or retreat to. Keep a routine as much as you can so that what happens next can be predictable for them.

3. Allow them to be a stranger to you at first.

It isn't personal. If they are friendly with you then embrace it but if it is taking time, then please be understanding. This is a completely unique individual that you are bringing into your life. Take the time to get to know each other. With rescues, many animals have been let down by humans. They don't know the circumstances that led to them leaving their original people and home. Some animals can be put out terribly. They don't have the ability to tell you they are afraid in words. The only way they can express they are upset and hurt is to show you behaviour, at least not until you can communicate with the animal. Having an animal communication can help immensely in understanding the point of view of the Animal.

> *For one horse in the US, a majestic being in stature he was upset. No one could ride him or even come close to him as he would kick and bite. Getting in touch with me was to see how he could be helped. All his new person wanted to do was ride him and give him a good life. He had bucked her off and kept his distance. I connected with this being and after introducing*

myself and finding out about him I asked about his life now and that I heard he was unhappy. He explained to me that he had no idea how he ended up here? Where was his person? Why did this happen? How long was he going to be here for? Is his person ok? He explained he didn't feel comfortable with the other horses where he was. What is going on? I explained to him what had happened. It was during Covid and unfortunately his mom had to go back to her country of origin in a hurry. Her neighbour took him. I let him know that his person was ok but sad to have left him. I shared with him his new person wanted to be a team player with him and possibly ride him, I shared that she was trying to understand him more and help him settle. When I asked what could help him he said to feel a sorry for not explaining anything to him would be good. I let his new person know what had been shared. A week later I received a message. His new person shared that she did apologise and as she stood there with his food bucket, this horse came behind her. She could feel his breath over her shoulder. With tears and gratitude, she reached back and stroked him. He let her, with each stroke, relaxed more. For 20 minutes they stayed like this, until he decided to move. After this interaction people including my client were able to approach and ride this being.

We can explain to the animals what is happening for them. We can reassure them of our intentions and that they are safe with us. Many animals show me how anxious they are in their new homes. Many of them are healing from the experience of being in a rescue or the ordeal of leaving their home that they have only known til now. Let your movements and intentions be gentle and slower so they can see what you are doing and get used to you.

4. Be aware of the energy that you bring.

This is relevant to any animal at any given time. Your energy can fill a room. You are the human and you can choose the energy that you bring to any circumstance or situation you are in. You can choose to be calm when you are with your Animal. Many animals that have stress or anxiety are influenced by their people. It can be a similar disposition with stress or anxiety between the both of you. Especially when they are new, let's be kind and do what can be done to ensure your energy is calm and safe for them. The rush of the mornings can be overwhelming for a new animal. Please reassure the animals. What if all could be calm in your exit? The calmer the energy, the safer your new animal feels.

5. Can't compare

It isn't fair to compare. This is a brand-new personality and your relationship is brand new as well. Nothing about this animal is to be compared to another animal. This being is here with their own purpose, their very own unique way of being and their own personality. For some animals, yes the soul can be one that your heart recognises from before and that is for your heart to know. Nothing else will be the same. For this animal there can be full acceptance for who they are. This is a brand-new relationship. The animals listen and take in what you are thinking. Be aware that they know when they are being compared to another animal.

In one conversation with a dachshund, I asked why it was that she charged at another dog that lived in her building. A poodle was simply minding her own business when my clients dog charged at her. When I asked, she replied that she heard her Mama talking just a few days before admiring the poodle and how easy going she was. She went on to tell me that she had heard her Mama say "I wish my dog was more like her." It was confirmed that these were the words said in this conversation.

Appreciate each animal for who they are. Many animals have shown me that they have been compared to previous animals that have been in the family. They have expressed to me that they feel they will never be good enough. We know how it feels to be judged and feel like we are never good enough as people. Animals have feelings too, so please be kind and have a fresh start with a new animal. Find out who this individual is, take the time to develop your relationship with them. Be their number one supporter and get help that you need from a place of love and not frustration. This animal has so much love to give you and if they feel safe and accepted you have all that love waiting for you.

6. Walkies and waiting

You may be excited to go on a walk with your new animal. Or it could be for the first ride on a horse. Go slow. Be kind. Ask first. If you see this as a team effort, then please take the time to see if they would like to go on a walk or a ride with you. Sometimes their time is different to our time. You can feel a yes from the animal and they will let you know when it is a no. Please wait for a yes. Now when you are walking, you may be disappointed at the difference to your previous animal. This animal may bound with excitement and may not have manners. All is fixable. Please be patient and set them up for success. Have clear kind boundaries and help them learn all about you and what you would like in your relationship.

7. Please be present on your walk with your animal.

Any animal at any given time, wants you all there. Give them time to sniff. Give them time to stop. Keep your phone out of sight. For a dog Bruce, he showed me his frustration with his Dad. Every night they would go on a bike ride together, only for Bruce it wasn't together. He had started pulling and not doing what he usually did when his Dad was on the bike. It interrupted his dad's ride. When I asked Bruce about it. He said he had started to do this because once he was attached to the lead and was running there was no more attention from his Dad. When I asked why he replied that Dad was on his phone while riding. No looking at Bruce. He would look up at his Dad as he was running. He said that he tried to ask him to stop. Bruce told me he had a click in his knee and that it had started to give him a niggle of discomfort. I let his person know. He hadn't noticed any limping from Bruce so was not aware. I let him know how Bruce felt disconnected from his Dad when they went for a ride. I also explained that Bruce would regularly check in by looking at him. Bruce's Dad now aware left the phone at home or in his pocket and made sure to check in with Bruce as they rode. He went slower on the bike and Bruce was thankful. He even mixed it up with sniffy walks. When I checked in after a few weeks, Bruce said he had stopped pulling in weird directions and was much happier with his Dad. He no longer feared being hurt as Dad looked at him often. All was confirmed by his Dad. The animals are grateful when the humans listen and make changes.

8. Talk to the Animals.

This always goes for all animals. Just talk to them out loud. They pay attention to your energy and your intentions mostly. We as humans use our words as a main way of communicating. This is good practice to say what you mean and mean what you say. Be a person of your word. Be a high value human. Be trustworthy for the animals. Be the person that always does what they say and communicate when something doesn't happen. Communicate when you are leaving the house, when you intend to come back. Any changes to the routine or circumstances let them know.

9. Don't pull or yank

When walking with your dog, please stop yanking. Ok I know that sometimes there are dogs that can totally forget their manners. Do what you can to learn how to be kind in teaching the animals how to walk. Be their teacher and their biggest support. Set them up for success. It can take time, so celebrate every win and set the intention that your walks are a pleasure. Your intention and the energy that you bring matters so much. The dogs can feel you through the lead and they can feel your energy. Frustration or fear can be felt by them so clearly. Let some walks be purely for sniffys.

10. If you wouldn't like it, chances are they wouldn't either.

It's not hard to figure out likes and dislikes. Pay attention to what you like and what you don't. It's key in understanding what the animals like and don't like. If it's a hot day and you wouldn't walk barefoot on concrete because it's too hot, then spare a thought for your dog's paws too. Just because they have a different texture to the bottom of our feet doesn't mean it doesn't feel hot for them. If the weather is hot, then please walk them when the sun is low. Early in the morning or in the late afternoon is kind. Your animals will be grateful. If you wouldn't like to be taken somewhere without explanation, your animals don't either. Tell them.

If you don't appreciate not knowing what is going on around you, your animals don't either. Tell them. If you like a heads up for change, be kind to the animals and let them know too.

11. Your words matter.

We don't always realise when the animals are listening or what they are listening to. No they aren't eavesdropping in on your conversations but when it has to do with them too, they listen.

In one communication with a frenchie gentleman, his person had contacted me as he had been taken to the vets multiple times, he no longer was eating. He was depressed and anxious and the vets did all kinds of tests. Nothing was found to be wrong. He was perfectly healthy. When I asked him what was going on he told me he was very worried. I asked why. He said he felt sick because his tummy was cramping. He hadn't eaten much at all. The acid in his stomach was churning. He was highly anxious and said that Mummy was talking about having a baby. He said she had said that HE was her baby. What would happen with him? When was this happening? All these questions came out from him. I asked if the conversation over the phone had happened in the kitchen one evening, two weeks ago? It was confirmed that yes it was. I asked if there was discussion about a baby and it was explained that they had a friend call to share their pregnancy news. This inspired the conversation about a baby for his people. I explained what was shared that he was their baby and he was very worried and upset. It all clicked! His mama got down on the floor and apologised to her boy and promised that he is always her baby and that if anything changes at all, she will always let him know. It was a heart felt sorry. He then showed me he was hungry. After a moment of cuddles on the floor, this boy simply got up and ate some of his food. He was back to his usual self. Over the next 2 days, he wanted to go on his walks again and his appetite came back. His mama is always aware of what she talks about around her boy.

12. Only nice names

Nothing hurts me more than to meet an animal whose human has hurt them with the names they call them.

For one dog who had a good and proper name, Henry, thought he had two names as his Dad called him the bastard. Henry showed me his Dad didn't look happy when he said his name. I let Henry know that was not his name and that it was not kind. Henry showed me the rest of his human family said his name with a smile and it felt very different to his Dad's name.

13. Put downs are out.

They know when you call them stupid or dumb and it hurts them. They know when you talk about them. They know when you are angry and they know when you are frustrated. Just because they might not understand you or do as you say, it doesn't mean they lack intelligence. For some it just doesn't make sense what you are asking. Or it can be too overwhelming. Or they don't listen to you because you aren't consistent or don't mean what you say. Be curious and find out why your animal doesn't listen. Always ensure that what you are thinking is aligned with what you are asking. Refrain from saying don't. Instead of don't dig up the garden, visualise them doing this at the beach happily or another activity that could be just as satisfying and say please stop digging.

14. Appreciate the love they show you

Not all animals appreciate the affection we would love to give. It can hurt us humans I know. We can feel rejected. I have had many people tell me how much they would love to cuddle their cat and all they wanted was to have a cat that loved to snuggle on them.

> *A cat that had been rescued by her new family, was keeping to herself, she wanted nothing to do with anyone and it was more than year later. The family didn't know what to do. When I communicated with this being she explained to me how everyone wanted her and it was all too much for her. The family had a 4-year-old child who loved to pick her up and carry her. She showed me wanting to just calmly walk to where she wanted to go in the house, only to be suddenly held*

up in the air. She was hiding and staying out of what this cat perceived as unsafe. I explained to the family what was stressing her so much, the volume, the high energy, the picking up and wanting to give her attention. I explained that this being wanted to have a choice and to give affection how she wanted to give it. I asked if the 4-year-old could calm her energy when near her and if she could sit quietly, perhaps the cat could come up to her and be allowed to leave when she chose. The family made some changes with the four-year-old doing her very best to be calm. This being felt much safer and appreciated not being picked up. It was happily shared that she came to sit with the daughter and no longer hides as she can move about freely and has a choice. Now she shows affection by her little rough tongued licks. It isn't how the family expected her to show her love but they accept.

15. Peeing or pooing is not a personal vendetta

Your animals peeing, whether on the floor, on your furniture or your bed is not personal. It's to let you know something. It could be the animal is not well. It could be picking up on residual smells. It could be territorial, illness or stress. It is for you to investigate what could be happening and why. You are the human in this relationship so communicate that you are not happy with it and see what you can do to help your animal.

With one female cat, she had three kitty litter trays around her home. She didn't use any of them. It was upsetting her family. Carpet had to be replaced, and something had to be done. I asked her why the peeing was happening, she showed me how big her home was. It was so big and overwhelming. She wanted to be in a smaller space like what I interpreted as a room and showed me the room which I described to her humans. They knew the space I spoke of was upstairs, it was an area that had a sitting area and an office. They made arrangements to have their beloved cat set up and a few days later I was messaged to let me know that there was no more peeing, and she seemed a lot more relaxed. I am happy to say that still there is no more peeing in the house and the family is happy.

16. The Animals have memories

The animals that have a past or have big event that happen such as big changes, injuries, accidents, losses or wrong treatment, the animals remember. They can't tell you that they have been triggered or that they remember something. Please be kind and acknowledge their fear. Please do what you can to help them. They don't know how to ask sometimes, so please give them love or a safe place to feel secure in.

For one mastiff in the US, he was an anxious being to the core. He showed me that he wanted to be in a crate but not closed. He showed me that big spaces were too scary for him, even though he was a decent size he found it overwhelming and preferred to be in charge of a much smaller space and a cozy den to retreat to. When I asked if something had happened, he showed me being left in a huge house all alone when he was little no food and water for days. He had a real fear from his life previously to his home now. His people gave him a crate and covered it for him as well as sectioning off a part of the house so his space didn't feel so big and overwhelming.

17. Explain what is going on at the vets

When you have an appointment with the vet or the groomers or any kind of treatment practitioner or specialist, let your animal know. Be the voice that explains what is happening. Be the calm they need. If you are nervous, they feel this too so please do what you can to be calm also. The animals just want to know they are safe and loved. If there is a procedure please tell them, if you are leaving them there, please also let them know and more importantly reassure them you are coming back to get them.

18. Being away from the animals.

It can be distressing for the animals to know that their people are going away or are away. They don't tell time but they understand when you let them know you are at work or going away on holiday somewhere. Talk to them the whole way through your planning if they are around while planning your holiday. If you are late from work, send a thought to let them know where you are and that you will be home soon. It's like a call but with your thoughts. Practice being aware of your thoughts and see if they pop in, if your animal does, that is not you. That is your animal sending you a message.

19. Silence can be loud

When you are leaving your animal at home during the day, be aware how empty and quiet home is when you are not there. Animals like to feel safe, most animals like some music playing quietly and a reassurance from you. If you have an anxious animal, please be calm and confident when leaving the house. Let them know you are coming back.

20. See with your heart.

With the older animals, look at them with eyes that see their strength and not their illness or weakness. Treasure them as they go through this stage. Slow down with them, give them all you can to say thank you for being the amazing animal they are.

21. Always ask

One golden rule that is always appreciated with the animals is to be asked. Be kind and ask your animal. Getting in the car? Ask them, do you need some help? Would you like some love from your animal? Ask, can I lay here with you? Can I pat you? Can I scratch you?

22. Trust your intuition

Be the advocate for your animal. Trust your intuition first always. No matter who says what, trust what your heart says first. Take your time in your responses. Give yourself time to connect to your inner wisdom when it comes to your animals. Your heart knows and it feels. Every single time, it knows what is true for you.

I hope you implement these tips as you interact with the animals around you. The animals are grateful every time they show me when their humans do these things with them. Be an example of a high value human with your animal. This encourages other people to recognise that the animals have feelings and matter. May this be inspiring in you being an amazing human being to your animal. May you see yourself how your animal sees the truth of who you are.

23. Be the calm in their storm

When your animal is afraid, do all you can to be their calm. It could be in a literal storm they really get scared. Maybe it is constant barking or pacing. Please do all you can to find out how to calm your animal.

For an anxious animal getting to a place of calm can be a real effort. You may want to investigate natural remedies that are gentle on their systems.

The first thing to remember is always how you are feeling. If you are stressed, this will only add to the situation. Do all you can to be calm. It could benefit you both to investigate nervous system regulation.

24. Rescues need rest and relaxation.

When you have a rescue animal come to your home, please give them clear direction as to where they toilet and where they sleep. For the first few days and up to a week, please allow them to approach you and give them space. No need for walks right away. Allow them time to settle in first and get used to the routine inside your home before you venture out for walks.

You have rescued them and always thank you but to them this is a new environment and scary. They don't know you yet and need time. The smells and sounds are all new and their nervous systems are overloaded. The kindest thing you can do, is to keep the environment predictable and calm.

Let them be introduced to the whole house slowly. Smaller environments feel safer, and they have time to let themselves get used the newness of it all.

It is also for you to be patient and kind in all ways, as you wait for your relationship to grow on trust.

I know you love your animals, and everyone does the very best they can with their animals. Please see this list as tips to help you be the very best human to them.

A 30 DAY JOURNEY WITH YOUR ANIMAL

This part of the book is for you if you would like to take the time to journal about your animal. As I said before it can be that journalling can be a meaningful way to remember your animal. To take the time to focus on them and to reflect can be an important part of healing.

Step 1.

To begin this journey, it is important that we begin with our intention. Our intentions are always what our animals know about us first. Our healing journey through grief begins with intention. You may want to release pain and regret as you write. Or perhaps you want to give yourself permission to feel all you do and be able to move through it all safely. Or maybe this is a sacred time for you to remember and honour the animal you loved. Take a moment to ask your heart what you would like to intend in completing this journal.

Step 2.

If you are going to do this, you can use the space provided or you can choose a notebook that will be a pleasure for you to write in. Choose a pen for this journey and have a place to put it when you are not using it. If it feels right for you, please have a candle to light for when you write your journal. Follow these prompts in your journal one day at a time. We will go gently through this journey. It doesn't take long to do. Be as peaceful as you can as you do this ritual for the next thirty days.

Step 3.

Please decide when you will do this practice. Is it in the morning before the household is awake? Is it a moment in the afternoon with a cup of tea? Or in the evening before you go to sleep? You decide when is best for you.

Step 4.

What will you do for yourself if you find that you are upset after a particular writing session? Let's come up with a plan. Please list five things you can do to bring comfort to yourself. It could be listening to a song, go for a walk, do a chore, visit a friend, or have a rest. What is it that you will choose to do? Keep it simple. Now that we have these things in place. Let's begin.

Day 1: My Animal

Choose a photo of your animal to print out. Choose one where you can see their eyes and one that makes your heart smile. The animals love when we remember them and smile. They want you to think of all the good memories that you have and the love that you share. It hasn't gone or disappeared, no matter the time apart, the love is always there. Under the photo on the first page, write their name and if it feels right, their date of birth or gotcha day and the date they transitioned.

Every time you sit down to write in this journal, your animal is asking you to look at their photo and invite them to sit with you as you write. It could be that you can feel them with you. Get curious. Every time you write with intention, take the time to look at their photo first.

____

____

____

____

____

____

____

Day 2: It's all in a name

How did your animal receive their name?

What nicknames did you have for your animal and what was your favourite?

____

____

____

____

____

____

____

____

____

____

____

____

Day 3: None other like you

Their personality and quirks made them uniquely who they are. What are some quirks about your animal? Describe their personality. If they were a person who would they be? Use your imagination. Look back at the photo if you like to help you in describing them.

Day 4: Our story

Take the time to write a story about your Animal's life with you. How did you find them? Write some key moments in your lives together.

Day 5: These are a few of my favourite things

Describe your Animal's favourite things to do. Describe their favourite toy.

Day 6: This was a favourite place

Write about your Animal's favourite place. Write about a memory you have with your animal in this place. It could very well be in your bed or at the beach. You choose one that makes your heart smile.

Day7: Oh you make me laugh!

What is your favourite funny memory you have of your Animal? Write about it. Bring yourself back there in your writing.

Day 8: Magic in the every day

What do you miss the most about your animal and what are you most grateful for? Gratitude helps to raise our vibration and makes it easier for the Animals to connect with us when it is time. To help with healing, it makes a difference to begin the day with gratitude.

____

____

____

____

____

____

____

____

____

____

____

Day 9: Keepsakes

What is the keepsake you are keeping from your animal and why? Write about the chosen keepsake and why it is important to you and what memories you think of when you look at or hold the keepsake.

Day 10: One Special Being

What role or purpose did your Animal fulfill in your life? The Animals can fulfill a few roles in our lives during their time with us. Choose the most important ones to you and how they fulfilled the roles.

Day 11: Forever isn't long enough

What will you do to remember your Animal on their eternity day? To keep count of the time from the day they left can mean that we hurt even more on the daily. What if you were to create a ritual for yourself to remember them by and mark this day especially, to consciously commemorate your Animal. To not count does not mean to forget. It means to allow it to be a part of your life now. It will never not have happened or never mean it didn't hurt, to not count means to accept and have acknowledged it all did.

____

____

____

____

____

____

____

____

____

Day 12: Dream a little dream of me

Have you had a dream of your Animal? Write about the dream. How did you feel? If you haven't dreamt of them as yet or you would like another dream, what would you like to experience?

Day 13: My words Matter

What are some affirmations you can tell yourself as you go through the journey of grief? Some affirmations may be, I am loved always. My heart is healing every day. My Animal connects with me with ease. I am open to signs from my Animal. What are some you can come up with that are just for you? Sometimes it helps to comfort ourselves or be our own cheerleader and reminder.

____

____

____

____

____

____

____

____

____

____

Day 14: Only Kindness Matters

How do you think your Animal would want you to show kindness to yourself? Write some things you can do that are acts of kindness or ways of being that are kind to yourself.

____

____

____

____

____

____

____

____

____

____

____

Day 15: Your Family

Who are in your Animal's family? What are their names and relationship to your Animal? Both animals and humans. Be descriptive as you can.

Day 16: If only it could have been different

Today is not an easy one and so I would like to choose something kind to yourself to do after this. Once you have chosen something then continue. Ok thinking of the last few weeks or days before your Animal left or perhaps throughout their lifetime, there may be things you wish could have been different, name them and write the reason why. This is acknowledging what is there and accepting that it all happened the way it did.

____

____

____

____

____

____

____

____

____

____

Day 17: They are right here with us too

Ask for your Animal to visit you. Write a heartfelt request to your Animal.

Day 18: If only I had one more day

What happened in their last days, write it all out, again this isn't easy but once we have acknowledged it and let it out, we can work on acceptance. After you have finished writing this, go and do something kind for yourself. Whatever you need to do.

____

____

____

____

____

____

____

____

____

____

____

Day 19: Say it again from the heart

What are some phrases you used to say to your Animal every day? They can still hear you if you say them. You can say them until you don't feel you need to anymore.

____

____

____

____

____

____

____

____

____

____

____

____

Day 20: I saw a sign and it opened up my mind.

Have you had a sign from your Animal? What was it? How did it happen? How did you feel?

____

____

____

____

____

____

____

____

____

____

____

Day 21: Helpers next to you.

Who do you reach out to when you need a friend or kind word? Why this person? What are you grateful for about this person?

Day 22: You are doing so well.

How do you feel you are healing? What are you doing to help yourself? Do you feel you are coming to a place of peace in your heart even if it hurts.

____

____

____

____

____

____

____

____

____

____

Day 23: Thinking forward

What will you do even better for and with the Animals moving forward? What are specific things you want to do differently in the future.

Day 24: Our heart can heal

How have you changed by having your Animal in your life? Write about what has changed through their life and in their transition. How has it changed you?

Day 25: I could be making this up.

We need your imagination for this one. Look at your Animals photo and have fun with this. What did you hear them say? Or what did they show you? First thought best thought, no take backs. Write it down. First thing that pops in.

____

____

____

____

____

____

____

____

____

____

____

____

Day 26: Can I have a treat?

Can you hear your Animal when they used to ask for a treat? Today they are asking if you can have a treat? What will you do today to treat yourself?

Day 27: How you feel matters

How are you feeling today? Reflect on your journey. Catch how you feel in this moment and make it a habit to regularly catch and name how you are feeling throughout the day.

Day 28: Gift of the Present

What gifts do you have from your Animal?

Day 29: Breathe Deep

What do you need to let be and accept today? Write it all out.

Day 30: What would you do?

If you could see your Animal one more time, what would you do? Describe where it would be and what you both would be doing?

We are at the end of the 30 day journal journey. Now I am going to ask you one last thing to do in this journal. I would like you to look at your Animals photo and I would like you to write a thank you letter from your heart to your Animal. Write it all out. All the thank you's out onto paper. Every single one. After you have finished, choose another photo of both of you and stick it in your journal. We are finishing this with gratitude and so when you look at your journal you will feel the gratitude you expressed in here. It can be anger and sadness, laughter and tears. All of it exists and felt because you are human and you have a heart. I hope this has helped you in your healing journey. Every time you think of your Animal you bring them back to you here. Ask your heart to help you know this truth. Your heart already knows.

CEREMONY

If you feel there is space for a ceremony or need a guide to create one. I offer one here for you or for family.

A Family Goodbye

A gentle ceremony to Honour an Animal together

Choose a time that feels right and gather together. Keep it simple.

Preparing Together

Have your children write a special note to your animal or do a drawing in preparation for this ceremony.

When it is time, place a photo of your animal in the centre of the room or on a table. Beside it, light a candle. You may like to also place their collar or their favourite toy and some flowers from the garden. Let children help to choose and arrange the space and items. Involving them helps them give their grief somewhere to land.

Opening the moment

Stand or sit in a circle.

Take one slow breath together.

You might say "We are here together because we love (insert your animal's name)." Keep your voice steady and calm.

Sharing one memory each

Invite each family member to share one memory or one thing they love about their animal.

It might be: I love how he waited at the door, I love how she slept on my bed. I loved walking with him.

If someone can't speak that is ok too. After each memory you can say gently 'Thank you (insert name)'.

Releasing Guilt.

If children are present this part is important.

You can something like 'Sometimes when animals pass away, we can wonder if we did anything wrong. Bodies get tired and when they do, it isn't because of something we forgot to do.'

You can ask if there is anyone that has a sorry in their heart that they would like to say to their animal. Comfort when needed.

Invite everyone to close their eyes

Ask for them to imagine your animal sitting in front of them and happy. Then say 'Imagine a soft thread from your heart to theirs. This is a connection for always. Love lives right here.

Final words

When it feels right, invite everyone to say together.

With love and gratitude thank you we say.

For the love and time that we shared through your life every day.

After the ceremony

You may want to create the altar as we discussed earlier or plant a flowering plant together. Or simply go and sit outside.

AFTERWORD

Here we are at the end of the book, and I hope this has opened your heart and mind to possibilities and curiosity for you with your animal. I hope it helped you feel what is true for you, in how you perceive and understand what happens with the animals in Spirit. I hope you know now by listening to what felt right in your heart, that your animal is very much happily here after. My wish for you is that you also know now without a doubt, that your animal loves you for always and that the bond of love that you share with your animals is for always and spans across all space and time. They are with you and the connection that you have with each other lives on and you will see them again! I hope you have curiosity and smiles when getting the signs from the animals. I hope you smile from your heart when you recognise that an animal has returned once more or an animal reminds you of your precious animal in Spirit.

May this book remind you of the animals in Spirit and all their love and bring to you a warm hug in words when you need it.

A heartfelt thank you for allowing me to be a part of your journey in healing and learning and for taking the time to read and take in what I shared.

The animals that are living with you now, are waiting for you to love them and honour them out loud and they can help you in your healing journey as you are hurting from the loss of your animal in Spirit. You too can help them heal as well.

Now you can see that each animal that comes to be with you has a purpose in being with you and you also with them. I hope there is even more love and appreciation that swells in your heart for your animal in Spirit, that came to be with you as they did. May there be even more gratitude and awareness of the precious animals in your life now as well. Perhaps you can also see, you have all you need within you, to keep this loving connection to come home to yourself and your animal. I hope that you give yourself permission to recognise you are always so much more than your body and thinking mind and you acknowledge the wisdom, magnificence and magic of your heart and soul as a part of you and your human experience from this point on.

ABOUT THE AUTHOR

Angèle Deane is an Australian animal communicator, author and intuitive guide, working with clients all around the world. Her work is heart centred- supporting people through grief and helping them trust their own intuition and connection with their animals both here and in Spirit.

Blending lived experience with years of professional practice, Angèle is known for her sensitivity and groundedness. Through her writing and communication work, Angèle bridges the worlds of connection, intuition and living from the heart into everyday life. She knows the connection we share with the animals continue in ways that are often subtle but deeply real.

She lives in Australia with her family and animals, writing and creating from a place of heart and compassion.

angeleconnections.com

facebook.com/angeledeane8

https://substack.com/@angeledeane

instagram.com/angele_connections